THE DECODED NEW TESTAMENT

The Decoded
New Testament

By Gene Savoy Sr.

VOLUME I OF A SERIES

The Sacred Teachings of Light

Codex II

THE DECODED NEW TESTAMENT

By Gene Savoy Sr.

Authorized Version

An Authoritative Translation of the Sacred Teachings of Light as Contained in the Encoded Writings of the Gospels, Acts, and Epistles.

International Scholar's Edition

Commentaries on Selected Writings of the Old Testament, Apocrypha, Pseudepigrapha, Early Christian Manuscripts, Scrolls, Fragments, and Other Ancient Religious Texts.

The International Community of Christ
Church of the Second Advent

PRINTING HISTORY
International Pulpit Edition Published 1974
Second Edition Published 1975
International Scholar's Edition Published 1977
Ebook Published 2021

Codex II – The Sacred Teachings of Light, Vol. I

Copyright © 1974 by Gene Savoy

All Rights Reserved. Copyright fuels creativity, encourages diverse voices, promotes free speech, and creates a vibrant culture. Thank you for buying an authorized edition of this book and for complying with copyright laws by not reproducing, scanning, or distributing any part of it in any form without permission.

Trademarks: The Second Advent Cross And Seal; "International Community Of Christ"; "Church Of The Second Advent"; "Jamilian"; And "Cosolargy" Are Registered Trademarks Of The International Community Of Christ.

ISBN numbers:
ebook: 978-1-949360-04-2
paperback: 978-1-949360-15-8

Published by the Jamilian University Press
ISBN: 978-1-94936

ALSO BY GENE SAVOY SR.

The Cosolargy Papers (12 Vols.)

The Academy Symposia (12 Vols.)

Project "X" Symposia (8 Vols.)

Antisuyo: The Search for the Lost Cities of the Amazon

On the Trail of the Feathered Serpent

Jamil: Child of Light

The Decoded New Testament

The Lost Gospel of Jesus

The Essaei Document

Prophecies of Jamil (8 Vols.)

The Book of God's Revelation

The Image and the Word (6 Vols.)

CONTENTS

1 Introduction

THE BOOKS OF THE DECODED NEW TESTAMENT

15 1. Humanity's Spiritual Genesis

25 2. Origins of the New Testament

41 3. The Loss of the Living Gospel

55 4. The Word: The Image of God

69 5. Mystery of the Divine Nourishment

93 6. Jesus Prophesies the Second Coming

111 7. Humanity's Immortal Nature

143 8. Christianity and God's Sun

159 9. Ancient Religions and the Sun

175 10. The New Birth

211 11. The Secret Church at Work

217 12. The New Revelations of Christ

NOTE FROM THE EDITORS

The author's original text from 1974 has been edited for inclusion, grammatical convention, simplified scriptural citation, and general readability. The author's use of the 1611 version of the King James Bible as reference text has been retained throughout.

Even though this book has been edited for inclusion, contemporary readers may balk at the author's use of the terms *Man* and *Mankind*, and so it may be useful to explain the author's intention when using these terms.

In the effort to render the English language gender-neutral in recent years, the words "human" and "humankind" are commonly and unthinkingly used to replace the words "man" and "mankind" because the word "man" in modern times is often used in a restricted sense to refer exclusively to males.

However, this narrowing of the meaning of *man* reflects a constriction of overall human thought. The word *man*—like Russian *chelovek* and German *Mensch* even today—originally designated all humanity, both men and women, as *thinking, intelligent beings*.

The Latin word *humanus*, from which we get out modern *human*, came into Latin completely separate from *humus*, meaning the organic constituent of soil, but the two terms are related. Along with the term *homo*, used in the designation of our species *Homo sapiens*, these words come from a form of the Proto-Indo-European word *(dh)ghomon-*, whose literal meaning is close to "earthling" or "being of the earth," earth here referring directly to dirt or soil. This association of humankind as a "being of earth" is widespread. Even the biblical story of the origins of humankind has life being breathed into a pile of dust. It is no coincidence that the first human is named Adam, from the Hebrew *adamah*, meaning ground.

As you will learn in this book, ancient prophets and philosophers taught that Man was made in the image of God, not as a physical being, for the physical body was related to the lesser nature of man, but as a Light body made in the image of the greater Light of God. This Light body was the archetype of Man—the true nature—from which evolved the physical form through some fault or transgression against God.

So while some readers might take exception to the use of the word *man* on the grounds that, at least in today's usage, it seems to exclude half the total number of sentient, thinking beings on the planet, we have decided to continue to use the original meaning of the English word, whose usage has been constricted and corrupted over the past ten centuries.

Hence we use the term *Man* with a capital *M*, not only in an effort to retain the association of the term with a divine as opposed to a material, earthly origin, but also to draw upon the original, uncorrupted meaning of the word *man* as a manifestation of "eternal Mind." For this reason, whenever you see *Man* with a capital *M*, know that this includes *you*.

And Christ the Lord shall enlighten thee,

the Sun of the Resurrection,

Begotten before the morning star

giving life by its beams.

Baptismal hymn used by early Christians, as cited in the Epistle to the Ephesians, 5:14; Psalms, 110:3; and the *Protrepticos* of Clement of Alexandria, Bk. 8, 84, 1–2.

INTRODUCTION

The announcement of God's Grace come into the world for the salvation of humankind and the means by which humans could share in it was given the name *Gospel* by the original Christian Community. The Gospel was of divine and not of human origin, as revealed through Christ. In the early period of the Christian communities, the Gospel of Christ was communicated orally from teacher to initiate exactly as received in the authentic tradition of Jesus, who had transmitted it to His original disciples. The Gospel could not be reduced to writing because it was a process that regenerated the individual in harmony with spiritual energies. Thus, the teacher was an agent of Christ who initiated other persons in the Gospel. The Gospel was always taught or applied in the community authorized and established by Jesus and therefore was a closed system. It was jealously guarded by the recipients in order to assure its continuation in original form and to prevent any alteration that might render the process ineffective. It was this compelling secrecy that eventually resulted in the loss of the Gospel when the original Christians were later martyred.

Today, Christians, being ignorant of the original Gospel of Jesus, tend to confuse it with the written Gospels recorded in the New Testament. It is a fact that our present-day Gospels were written at a later date, long after the original teachers or transmitters of the Gospel were no longer available to the Christian communities.

Even the original scrolls used as a blueprint for our own Gospels were recorded by individuals who interpreted the Gospel from the remaining oral traditions, which included the so-called Gospel sayings or sources. These Gospel sayings or sources, many of which were altered according to the individual transmitter, were in existence during the early days of the Christian ministry and were used as the basis for the original written Gospels, which have since disappeared. These latter documents served as the sources for the Gospels of the New Testament.

Because of the complexity of the history of the Gospels, and of the New Testament in general, we must first accept that the earliest Gospels—or the original scrolls containing sayings of Jesus—were used as manuals, which were read by the ordained to the community and were always interpreted orally by someone familiar with the unwritten Gospel of Jesus.

Therefore, not being in possession of the original, unwritten Gospel, which is a means of salvation through God as given by Christ, the Christian Churches today are not representative of Christ's message. What we know as the Christian religion is composed of a multitude of Churches that speculate on the original Gospel and confine themselves to faith, theology, myth, and history.

The classical beauty of biblical scripture, both the Old and the New Testaments, is not to be doubted. Biblical scripture represents some of the most inspiring literature possessed by humankind. Moreover, it is a testimony of the prophets and holy teachers of time past.

The Bible is a varied collection of sixty-six books, excluding the Apocrypha, written over a period of a thousand years. The New Testament, written from the last half of the first century to the end of the fourth century, is a collection of twenty-seven books, which represent diverse opinions. The first four books, called the Gospels (Matthew, Mark, Luke and John), tell the story of Jesus' birth, infancy (in part), His teaching and ministry, His death and resurrection. The remaining twenty-three volumes, consisting of the Acts, Epistles, and, finally, the Book of Revelation. The Old Testament was written almost entirely in Hebrew. The New was written mostly in Greek and carried on the Hebrew tradition, accepting that Jesus was the long-awaited Messiah who had come to establish God's Kingdom on Earth.

The Gospels and the New Testament writings do not contain the whole teachings of Jesus, who delivered them orally to His own disciples. Scholars have known for some time that many of the writings attributed to Jesus were never spoken by Him but were fabricated by the later compilers of the Gospels. Catholic Christianity has always taught that the Church and its tradition took priority over the Bible. Scholars knew of the imperfections of the Christian writings, but the laity did not. It was for this reason that the Church kept the writings away from the masses, because it knew that distribution of the writings could bring about heresy and schisms. With the invention of the printing press, the Bible became available to the laity for the first time. Up to that time, the writings had been confined to a relatively select group. Luther brought about the Protestant Reformation with his Justification by Faith, supported by the Bible and its use by all Protestants.

What we find in New Testament writings is a fragmentary record of the life and teachings of Jesus. Much of this information is contradictory. The differences between the Synoptic Gospels (Matthew, Mark, and Luke) and John's Gospel are enormous, as every scholar knows. Shrouded in cryptic symbology, the teachings of Jesus are all but lost to the reader. The earliest manuscripts date from the fourth Christian century. The original manuscripts, those older source scrolls, have not survived. We only have copies. We can assume that many assertions were made by later writers who were not in touch with the earliest writings and were ignorant of the oral teachings transmitted by Jesus to the early Christians.

Jesus was an inspired man of God who sought to amend the Hebrew religion. The learned scribes and rabbis were disturbed by this and brought Him to trial before their religious council, the Sanhedrin. The Sanhedrin convicted Him of blasphemy because His authority was based on His own teachings and not upon written Scripture and the established oral tradition of Israel. Though Jesus honored the prophets and upheld the Law, He nevertheless claimed authority to bring about the fulfillment of the Hebrew religion. He did not claim to be the Messiah or King of the Jews, except in a spiritual sense. His efforts to amend the Hebrew religion were sufficient to eventually bring about His judicial murder.

The resurrection of Jesus is the basis of Christianity and assumes far more importance than the message of the New Testament, which is a message of good will and brotherhood. Jesus demonstrated the spiritual nature of humans to show humankind that all are immortal creatures made in the image of God. This message was to be announced to all through the disciples Jesus ordained. The disciples were His representatives or ambassadors; they were evangelists, or "heralds of the good news."

The cosmic truth of Jesus extended to humankind a reunion with God and was above the Law and the prophets. Indeed, Jesus was sent to alleviate a suffering humanity. Jesus taught a system through which all humankind could attain spiritual immortality. The message of Jesus was not human-inspired, but was revealed directly from the mouth of God, as Jesus was a divine and preexistent being representative of the Godhead. Salvation was made possible through the grace of God manifesting to the world through a cosmic phenomenon. Since this cosmic salvation was a divine event, it was superior to and beyond that of the man Jesus. God, not Jesus the teacher, was the Redeemer; Jesus was the messenger who announced the prophetic revelation and the proper means by which a righteous humankind could participate in its own divinity.

Paramount in this revelation was the promise of a renovation of the old world and the birth of the new. The righteous would triumph over the wicked and evil powers, and the Messianic Kingdom under God would be established forever. The event did not take place because the message of Jesus was lost soon after His crucifixion. Humankind failed to participate in the cosmic plan and attain fellowship with God as did Jesus. Thus the Light went out.

Jesus preached the fulfillment of a common tradition known in different forms throughout the world. This tradition was partially preserved by a sect of the Jews, the Essenes, with whom Jesus was familiar. The origin of this tradition can be traced to all ancient civilizations far back into time. The Jews were by no means the first to possess this tradition; they may have been exposed to it during the Egyptian oppression or later under the Babylonians, Persians and Greeks. Whenever this tradition is extended to a people, it is accompanied by the birth of a World Teacher, such as Jesus, who amends and supplements the older tradition.

The idea of a World Redeemer was not unique to Christianity; that is, that teaching that spread out of Palestine and that we call *Christianity*; it was Greek in origin. The *Christos*, the son of God, was derived from a solar theology. He was the fruit of heaven created by the marriage of heaven and earth and conceived by the spring sun (fire) and rain (water). He was destined to save the world and, above all, to save people's souls. Humankind was to become regenerated through the *gnosis,* or knowledge, of God as taught by the prophets of God. When the Christian message was preached abroad and non-Jewish people, or Gentiles, were attracted and converted to the new faith, it came to grips with these older teachings.

Many saviors had come long before Jesus, and many of the teachings the early Christians believed original and unique were as old as the Gentile world. Other savior-gods included Mithra, Adonis, Attis, and Osiris. The Iranian Zoroaster, like other saviors, was born of a virgin mother, and his coming was heralded by a star and other heavenly signs. The Syrian Attis, like Adonis, was killed by a boar beneath a pine tree and was laid to rest in a sepulcher. When night had fallen the darkened tomb burst into celestial light and the god stepped forth resurrected, promising salvation for his adherents in a fashion similar to his own. This divine resurrection was celebrated on the twenty-fifth day of March, the vernal equinox. A hymn to Attis reveals his universality:

> *Whether thou art the offspring of Kronos or, blessed one, of Zeus or of great Rhea—hail, Attis, at whose name Rhea looks down. The Assyrians call thee thrice-lamented Adonis; all Egypt, Osiris; Greek wisdom, the heavenly horn of the moon; the Samothracians, venerable Adamnas; the Haemonians, Corybant; and the Phrygians, sometimes Papas, sometimes Corpse or God or Sterile or Goat-herd or Harvested Green Sheaf or Flute-player whom the Fertile Almond brought forth.*

Hippolytus, Ref. v. 9. 8

Such ceremonies were celebrated at Rome on Vatican Hill, near the present site of the great Basilica of St. Peter and also at other places. The ceremonies included a sacramental meal where the initiate was regenerated in a new birth, and the remission of sin was achieved by the shedding of a bull's blood. Since Attis was killed by a boar, they abstained from eating pork.

The Persian savior-god Mithra fought on the side of the God of Light and came to the earth from the sun. His followers participated in a sacred meal of bread and wine, performed baptism, and believed in a creed of salvation and in high morals. The sun often sent messages to Mithra on rays carried by a raven, and his sign was a rock. His birth date was the twenty-fifth of December, according to the Julian calendar. This date, the end of the winter solstice was also recognized as the nativity of the sun, which after lying still for three days, began again its ascent northward. Like Osiris, he was likened to an infant. Upon his death, Mithra was supposed to have ascended into heaven.

The teachings of Mithra among the Romans were so strong that the Christian Church adopted the birthday of Mithra as the birthday of Jesus and discontinued the sacred Sabbath day of the Jews in favor of the Mithraic first day of the week (Sunday), the day of the Conquering Sun. The Last Supper, or Eucharist, as it was known in Mithraism, was taken over by the Christians as a sacrament and blended with the Jewish sacred meal. The blood of the lamb and the atonement for sins recalls the Mithraic rite in which the adherents were washed clean by the blood of Taurus, the Bull.

Among the Latins and the Teutonic peoples, persons who had offended their gods were sacrificed, or consecrated, to the gods by being hung on a tree and wounded or pierced in the side with a spear. Jesus was crucified on a stylized tree because He had offended Jehovah and the Roman deities.

The Jewish law held one to be accursed who was hung on a tree:

> *If a man have a stubborn and rebellious son, which will not obey the voice of his father, or the voice of his mother, and that,*

when they have chastened him, will not hearken unto them:

Then shall his father and his mother lay hold on him, and bring him out unto the elders of his city, and unto the gate of his place;

And they shall say unto the elders of his city, This our son is stubborn and rebellious, he will not obey our voice; he is a glutton, and a drunkard.

And all the men of his city shall stone him with stones, that he die: so shalt thou put evil away from among you; and all Israel shall hear, and fear.

And if a man have committed a sin worthy of death, and he be to be put to death, and thou hang him on a tree:

His body shall not remain all night upon the tree, but thou shalt in any wise bury him that day; (for he that is hanged is accursed of God;) that thy land be not defiled, which the LORD thy God giveth thee for an inheritance.

Deuteronomy 21:18–23

Though a tree or cross was used to hang criminals on in Roman times, in more ancient times the tree was worthy of bearing a savior. The tree was a symbol of life itself; being rooted in the underworld, its branches stretched heavenward like the Sephiroth Tree of the Kabbalah, having roots above and below. The ancient Adonis was born of a tree. Buddha was enlightened under a tree. Attis died under a tree. The central tree of the Garden of Eden gave to Adam and Eve the fruit of knowledge. The pine tree held the body of Osiris and was used as the central pillar in the Temple of Byblos. The tree stood at the crossroads of the world; an Axle-Tree of the Upanishads and the Bhagavad-Gita, growing out of Brahma, the Sun. Odin hung himself upon the World-Tree, Yggdrasil, as recorded in the Rune Song of Odin:

I know that I hung on a wind-rocked tree nine whole nights, with a spear wounded, and to Odin offered myself to myself; on that tree of which no one knows from what root it springs.

Osiris, a sun god (or God of the Sun) who, like Jesus, was born in a cave, was symbolized by a tree trunk with a cross beam. He was a vegetative god of regeneration who died for his people and was reborn. His followers believed that through him and by his name they would awake from death to live eternally with him. The Egyptians believed in Osiris for thousands of years before the birth of Jesus. Resurrection of a god was nothing new to them.

Many of the teachings which came to be accepted as Christian were not original with Christianity at all; indeed, they were not even claimed by the early Christians. The concept of a virgin birth was known among the Mediterranean peoples at a very early date, long before Jesus was born. The idea began with the Virgin Earth Goddess who received the seed from the Sun, and the fruit of her womb was the spring growth. Her son was born, lived, died, and was entombed in the earth only to be reborn the following year. This concept had a parallel among the ancient Sun Priests who taught that the Virgin Sky Mother, Virgo, was impregnated by the Sun itself when the constellation rose in the eastern sky with the appearance of the star Sirius, heralding the birth of a New Sun.

Many of the ancient religions, like Zoroastrianism, taught that a final age of the world would dawn; the Messiah (Saoshyant) would come on the last day of judgment, all evil in the world would be destroyed, and a new world would be created by Ahura Mazda, God of Light. It was because this idea was ingrained in the minds of the many peoples of Western Asia and Europe (but by no means restricted to them) that Christianity, with its message of a newborn savior teaching universal fellowship and peace on earth, was embraced by so many. Similar ideas were known in other parts of the world as far east as India, China and even in the Americas. When the Spaniards conquered the Indians of Mexico and Peru, they found a resemblance to Christianity in a religion which taught that a Redeemer who walked the Americas in ancient times healed the sick, made the blind see, and taught a religion of peace that included ethical teachings comparable to those of the Christians.

The above examples of religious ideas resembling those of Christianity introduce the question of synthesis: was Christianity original, or did the Church absorb older concepts in an effort to build a universal religion? As Christianity spread outward into the civilized world, it encountered doctrines of a Redeemer who was the Son of God. To the Judaic Christians, Jesus was the Messiah, a Messenger from God come to establish a new world order. The idea of atonement by blood was entirely foreign to the early Christians. So was the idea of a savior god-man. Can we assume that existing salvation cults influenced the early Church as it grew and developed in the world of the Gentiles? Of great interest to us is the similarity of the life of Jesus with that of previous saviors. Are the stories of His life actually true, or did they draw on already existing stories attributed to earlier Redeemers? If the stories of Jesus' life are authentic, why do they resemble the lives of earlier teachers?

Jesus was judged and condemned by orthodox Jewry because of His innovations upon the living tradition of Israel. The Jews saw only the human nature of Jesus, discounting the fact that He was also the image of God sent from on high. In their judgment of the man they rejected the redeeming gift of God. Jesus, who held the title of Christ, was overshadowed by the great Light radiated by God. But they did not see this Light, having been under the Law for so many centuries and removed from God's Light and grace, they could not see that God could communicate to them through Christ. They could not see that the Jewish community could have held the title of Christ collectively as did the man Jesus individually, thus serving as messengers to the world, imitating the Teacher. And so, as a nation, they failed to see this Light.

The Palestinian Jews were convinced that Ezra (465–424 BC) was the last of the inspired prophets, and that no sacred Scripture written after him could be included in the canon of scripture. It was this belief more than any other that resulted in the rejection of the ministry of Jesus by the larger part of Israel. A fixed or static condition is always crippling to any great world religion.

Much the same can be said of modern Christianity. All too often the idea of Christ is confined to the pages of scripture. The canon of scripture has been considered fixed and inviolable for many centuries, even though the doctrine of inspiration varies with certain New Testament texts. Be this as it may, any effort on the part of an individual to disturb the contents of the canon would be considered blasphemous or heretical by the Church. This is as it should be, except when change is by divine inspiration directly from God.

The purpose of the *Decoded New Testament* is to clarify the cryptic message hidden in the encoded writings of the New Testament. We have emphasized that the Gospel writers worked from ancient scrolls and the oral tradition of the Gospel. Both of these sources were in allegorical form in order to keep the Gospel message hidden, and it is this cryptic symbology that has confused the Gospel message over the centuries.

Every Christian is entitled to become familiar with the oral tradition of the living Gospel as part of his or her Christian heritage. The Gospel cannot be fully explained by the written word. All we can do in the present text is to explain the long history of the Gospel, how it was given, lost, and finally repossessed in modern times. A reading of the *Decoded New Testament* is the first step in acquainting the reader with the "Good News."

The Gospel is still being transmitted orally by the ordained to the initiate as has been done for thousands of years. Only in this way is the Gospel message fully understood and applied. Therefore, the *Decoded New Testament* is used as a scriptural text by those being initiated into the Gospel. Without the oral teaching, the value of the *Decoded New Testament* is diminished.

The International Community of Christ has decoded the New Testament as a needed service to Christendom. The decoding serves to familiarize the average Christian with the Gospel so that more serious studies can be made at a later date. The *Decoded New Testament* gives the Gospels and Epistles new meaning without which the Gospel message of Christ cannot be grasped. Once it is understood, the Christian comes into repossession of the message of Christ, the Gospel, and begins the work as outlined by Christ.

We now consider the Community's authority: the lost Gospel message could only be restored by Christ, since it is not of human origin. That the Christian communities would fall under apostasy— i.e., lose the Gospel message—was predicted by the Christian prophets. That Christ would come again at a later age to restore and amend the message was the great promise of Jesus. The reestablishment of God's Kingdom on Earth was also promised: This will be the goal of the future Church of the Second Advent, as this goal was not realized by the Church of the First Advent.

The International Community of Christ was founded by Christ come in the image of a little Child, the full story of which is the subject of Codex I, Sacred Teachings of Light, presently in the possession of every community member. The Christ Child lived for a period of three years, then returned to the Worlds of Light from which He had come, but not before restoring the Gospel message and revealing a new Christ Age extended by God for the redemption of humankind. Though skeptics may doubt that Christ has appeared in modern times or that He could come as a little Child, it is the repossession of the Gospel and its power to regenerate the individual in harmony with God that authenticates His Coming. Therefore, it is not a matter of faith alone, but of personal experience that validates the Coming.

Christianity shall be altered by this Coming as were the established religions with the coming of Christianity. The result shall be a new universal teaching that shall bind humankind into a cosmic order of greater dimensions than ever believed possible by a searching humanity. This universal teaching shall reach far beyond the limitations of dogmatic or theologizing religions because it is instructing individuals in how to experience Christ and live a life of righteousness in fellowship with God.

By these means, it shall unite the human race everywhere into a truly universal fellowship guided by the Holy Spirit moving within its midst. Its followers are pledged to exemplify Christ in their daily lives, thereby sustaining the Spiritual Sun of Righteousness for the establishment of a new world under God.

Above all, they are dedicated to keeping the living Gospel alive for the salvation of the human family.

Gene Savoy Sr.

May 23, 1974

1: HUMANITY'S SPIRITUAL GENESIS

There existed in the ancient world, long before our written history, a Great World Religion common to all races. The tenets of this Religion taught that humans are endowed with highly refined spiritual faculties and that their descent is traced, not to earlier animal forms, but to spiritual beings in realms remote from the physical world. The human intellect and psyche are the outgrowth of a God Consciousness. The physical organism is the outgrowth of a spiritual Light body. Man's emergence on the planet was not accidental but the result of a preexistent nature.

Being the descendant of a Primordial or Archetypal Man no longer with us, Man is the oldest living creature on the planet, the degenerate offspring of a supra-man that was half spiritual, half physical. Human spiritual faculties, oftentimes repressed through lack of knowledge, indicate this.

To understand the history of the world and the nature of humanity, we must go back to the beginning when all was Light, and the Angels of Light walked with God in fellowship, perfect and immortal.

The following passages taken from the manuscript of Codex VI, 10:1–38 of the Sacred Teachings of Light, now in the possession of the International Community of Christ, describe humanity's beginning in the Worlds of Light and descent into the physical world:

> *But the Angels turned from God and their world changed like a blazing star fallen from the heavens. And it heaved and shook like a glowing coal cast from the fire. The great invisible light slowly diffused, being neither visible nor invisible. Made in the image of God di, the Angels took on new form, scattering their spirit into the new creation. And pure life became splintered and imperfect. And the Angels became ignorant of God Sk. And sin was born, which is to say, the Angels fell from the grace of God e by living in error.*
>
> *It was as if a disobedient child flew from the sanctuary of its father's house and the love of its mother, only to find itself alone in a new world without guidance. And the Angels were alone, cut off from the benevolent Parent. And the consciousness of the Angels given by God longed for unity with the Greater Consciousness of God. And the Angels began to recreate, as best they could, the life they had known before.*
>
> *And so it was that the Angels remembered the beginning, and they were reunited with God, becoming perfect again. But with the renewal of their spiritual beings, some of the Angels developed a new sense, a sense of self-beingness, and they boasted of their equality with God. And the Angels were empowered by the Light of their own being, believing that they were self-sufficient. They were plunged into the darkness of their own creation, cut off from the Greater Light eft by their own arrogance. This was the second fall, and that darkness was greater than the first. And the World of Darkness thence came into being. Being creatures of God, the Dark Angels reproduced themselves and they inherited a new world, being not of the Light if, but more of an ethereal nature.*

But their immortal nature became mortal, as the Light diffused even further. Their invisible bodies of Light became more opaque, taking on a new form. Something that had never occurred before took place as the Angels of Darkness diffused and their once perfect form and being faded. This was the first death.

Life in this new world continued. And there occurred a coming and going, as life came into being only to fade, for they were not self-sufficient being cut off from the Greater Light of God. And they did live off the energy generated by their own beings. And this caused death; and they became conscious of time, something they had never known before. Forms decayed into matter, and their world was built up of visible light and energy. And they became conscious of space, as form was removed from the ethereal realms. And a whirlwind of form and spirit pressed upon their bodies and they were conscious of weight for the first time. And so it was that Man came into being, descended from the Angels of Darkness and the Angels of Light before them, made in the image of God, now diffused into matter—a mortal creature—visible, made of sinew, flesh and bone.

And perceptory senses of their material bodies responded to the new creation, and First Man experienced his world. Gradually, Men forgot the first creation and the second creation. Life became a myriad of living things.

But the spirit of God was within their being and the echo of greater beingness stirred within, and some remembered.

And God, hearing the call of Man, sent an Angel into the world to teach Men, for they were the generated beings of God; their spirit was immortal in spite of their new-born mortal natures. For the spirit of God is the cause, and all life, from the lowest to the highest, always seeks a return to the source from whence it came.

And Man was moved to remembrances of his divine nature by the Angel of God, but his earthly nature was dense and he could not see or hear its words. And he was troubled and disturbed, being agitated from within.

And a second time God did seek to speak out to Man. And He incarnated in an earthly Man; the divine blended with the human nature, and the Great Man, holding the office of Christ, the mediator between Man and God, formulated a proper path to immortality in the Godhead. And many Men did hear and were saved by the grace of God. And the world experienced an Age of Light And the true religion, which teaches man of his divine nature and the means of attaining union and fellowship with God was possessed for the first time.

And the world would have been restored to Light, but the human natures of Men became allied with Dark Angels who visited the earth and conspired against God and the Christ Being come among them. The Dark Angels, hoping to consume the Great Light of His Being, did kill Him, and did eat His body. Such is the nature of Man's self-beingness inherited from the Dark Angels.

And the world was plunged into darkness greater than ever before. And the sphere did experience terrible cosmic upheavals. And the stars did fall from heaven, and the Sun was darkened. And the earth grew cold.

Man entered the depths of the earth where he lived for a great age without benefit of Light from heaven. And the world became hostile; Man was an alien with all life conspiring against him. And he was afraid and called out to the God he remembered in the spirit of his being.

And the Sun did shine again to warm the planet. And Man came forth to claim the surface of the earth as he had in past ages.

Time passed and the earth flowered. And Man reproduced himself covering the earth once more with his offspring.

And when the earth was fruitful Man called out to God. And God did incarnate in a Holy Man who walked the earth, teaching the arts and sciences of the True Religion.

But the Dark Angels conspired against Him and again the world was plunged into darkness for the third time.

And the cycle repeated itself four times. Influenced by the Powers of Darkness, Man lost sight of the redeeming salvation of God's grace by failing to live the life intended for him that promised the restoration of the world to Light as it had been in the beginning.

Governed by differences in environment and the struggle to survive, Men differed from one another in stature and color, and were separated by continents, mountains and seas.

And again Man yearned for enlightenment, for his suffering was great. And God heard him and inspired Holy Men in distant parts who recalled the Holy Teachings. And mankind did listen to the teachings, for they were fearful that another catastrophe would visit the earth as it had done before.

And in time, the tribes and nations of the earth prospered and multiplied. And they roamed far and wide by land and by sea. And Holy Men did bind them together into a great universal civilization. And they worshipped God and the Light and did absorb these powers into their very beings, and became as godly as men ever have.

And the Kings of Earth formed a Sacred Brotherhood under the Word of God. And each was sworn to guard the ancient teachings. And in those days the Kings did abide by the advice and counsel of the Holy Men who formed an order of tradesmen, artists, philosophers, healers, agriculturists, herdsmen, craftsmen, astronomers, mathematicians, builders and engineers: all formed part of a whole teaching as governed by the True Religion. And all labored for the overall good of the world and for God. And no one gave thought to personal gain.

And their cities and Holy Places were erected in such a way as to reflect the cosmic/solar forces, radiating from the sun and the stars, back into space and thence to Godhead. And they did fill the returning light forces with love and goodness.

And the earth sparkled like reflected moonlight on a calm sea. And for a time all was well.

But the Holy Ones, knowing that the earth and earthly bodies of mankind were imperfect, impermanent and mortal—for death was still with them—sought to direct them back to the source of their being.

And they did teach the Kings and peoples of the earth that all must be transformed back to Light. For only in spirit would they be truly perfect, permanent and immortal. And they were asked to detach themselves from the material world and to cease reproducing themselves. And the path was difficult, for men, now bound to the material senses and the material pleasures, found it not easy to transform themselves back to Light.

And many of the learned ones did dispute with the Holy Ones. They saw no need for such sacrifice. Indeed, if mankind accepted the teachings of the Holy Ones, it would mean the extinction of society and the termination of the human race. Had they not mastered the powers of the terrestrial forces? Had they not fused these forces with celestial forces? Did they not control the very forces of life itself living to great ages in reasonable health and abundance?

And some of the Kings hesitated to enforce the decisions of the Holy Ones who had guided them in all things.

And the seed of rebellion was sown. And a schism came to pass. Kings of the provinces separated from the Great Brotherhood into independent nations. And those sworn against the Holy Ones formed a confederation. And the Holy Ones spoke out against them, warning of ultimate disaster if they proceeded.

And evil Kings did imprison the Holy Ones, disregarding their warnings that the natural environment was vulnerable to disaster if God and the Light were neglected in favor of material pursuits.

And the goodly Kings sought to free the Holy Ones and re-establish the Holy Order of the world. But the evil Kings refused, threatening to misuse their technical skill of nature, turning it to destructive powers against their opponents, if necessary. Thus the temptation of the Powers of Darkness grew in man once more. And many of the Holy Ones were killed.

What had once been unthinkable became a reality. The great races of the earth separated into factions and warred against one another. And great was the destruction. And the balance of nature was upset and cataclysms befell the inhabitants of the earth.

And again the earth was depopulated and anarchy and chaos reigned. The Great Age of the earth vanished.

And the survivors abandoned the Holy Places and ruined cities, migrated to new lands, taking with them their spiritual secrets and oral traditions. And those that applied this knowledge prospered. But always they were at the mercy of ignorant tribes and nations bent on destruction and material aggrandizement.

And the knowledgeable peoples of the earth died out, and their sacred writings, inscribed on the sacred scrolls and tablets, remained a mystery to those that inherited them.

And men gone astray lost their control over natural events, becoming like dumb animals, pitiful creatures, victims of the fury of the elements. Cut off from the order of a Godly rule, men existed in a world of disorder governed by natural phenomena combined with the cosmos unleashed in a series of events that threw fear into their very souls. Celestial objects showered down upon them in unending display.

And the Holy Places built by the ancients on sacred ground, now unattended by Holy Ones, generated lines of light heavenward. Man was governed by fear of the strange events visiting the earth. And luminous spheres did streak across the heavens to and fro, seen as fireballs by their observers. And man experienced strange dreams.

And superstition was born in the hearts of the inhabitants. And the storytellers, drawing from ancient Holy Writings, told tales of the past. The old cosmic saviours became mythical figures and part of man's folklore. And men did fall down and worship these phenomena and the beings that manifested in them. And profane religions resulted from these magical animations.

Such were the events that shaped the minds of what we call prehistoric humans. It was within that environment that the present race, having experienced numerous mutations, has its roots.

God has never failed to send inspired ones to awaken humankind to its spiritual heritage. Holy Prophets of God have taught within the last seven thousand years of humanity's present cyclic age, which is nearing its completion. All Holy Teachers have taught spiritual insights that humans find difficult to fathom by virtue of their perceptory senses. Kings and rulers of the earth who have set themselves up as lords over the lives and destinies of other people without regard to humanity's spiritual nature or the need of the world to harmonize with the Worlds of Light have sought to suppress the Holy Teachings for the "good of society" on the grounds that they teach against established religions, rule, and order. Such kings and rulers do not know that they ally themselves with the old enemies of humankind: the Powers of Darkness that seek to keep humanity from its spiritual heritage, and hence bring about the further degradation of the human spirit and the cataclysmic end of the world.

With this summary of the world's cosmology, the reader is now in a more favorable position to undertake a comprehensive examination of scriptural writings of the New Testament and the inner teachings of Jesus, which, unbeknown to Christians, have not come down to us.

2: ORIGINS OF THE NEW TESTAMENT

The New Testament is not a document that relates the historical life of Jesus and that was dictated by God and handed down to us in its original, pure form. Biblical scholars are well aware that it developed out of a collection of writings, which in their present form cannot be dated earlier than from the end of the first and into the second centuries of our era. The writings, including the Gospels, underwent editorial revisions, alterations, and additions by numerous redactors who changed the meaning of the message. At one time, in the history of the early Christian Community, the writings were used as manuals of religious instruction that needed additional oral instruction to be complete; oral teachings that have since been lost.

Scholars, as well as clergy, can only speculate on what this oral instruction was. They know that the New Testament is much more than a historical document (which seems to be important to the Christian religion, which stresses the need for faith in the truth of the episodes told in its pages) and that it somehow taught an experience outside the perceptory senses of the physical mind/body.

Long before anything was ever put into writing in the early Christian community, a living Gospel existed and was passed down orally from one person to another. The writings came much later and were based on that portion of the living tradition known to the compilers. The written texts that later served the interests of the organized Church, which stressed theology, were never primary. It was the secret oral tradition that remained paramount. This living Gospel became garbled as it was handed down from teacher to student. With countless retellings it became a romance mingled with legends and the folklore of the peoples who told it. Jesus, the Messiah, took on the qualities of the many salvation gods known to the peoples throughout the Mediterranean area. It was this living Gospel that served as the Logia, or Secret Sayings, which inspired the Gospel writings. The original documents have not come down to us, but we know from close examination of the writings that the sayings, which were shrouded in cryptic symbology to disguise the true message, were later rationalized by writers who did not understand the terms. As a result, they were prepared as historical and biographical accounts, accepted literally and steeped in dogmatic teachings that served the interests of the organized Church, which was interested in discipline, worship, and theology. This explains why all Christians of the first and second centuries did not accept the written Gospels with which we are familiar.

Jesus never wrote down His teachings. They were given orally to the disciples, who took an oath to hand them down exactly as received, and only to the sworn members of the Order, but never in written form. As a result, the writers of the earliest documents used coded cryptography and allegory to disguise the real meaning of the teachings.

The oral teachings, passed from the master to the disciple as received, linked the communicant with Jesus directly. It was not a teaching learned from the written Gospel or from any of the many manuals or books of instruction. It was something that each experienced for himself or herself under the guidance of a teacher ordained by Christ. The idea that one could experience the new life, which resulted from participating in the original teachings, by a mere reading of scripture would have been unthinkable to an early Christian.

Oral communication of the Gospel was not only the earliest means of transmitting the teachings of Jesus as revealed by God, but the one authentic means; it made possible the new man or woman in Christ, who participated in the living ministry of Jesus and enjoyed fellowship with God as divine beings.

Theology, dogma, worship, faith, and belief in written scripture itself is of no more value to the true Christian than it would be for the Jew to adhere to the laws of the old dispensation. Christians should be involved in the regeneration that comes from participation in the divine plan as Children of God. To accomplish this, a new birth is necessary. It is as real as physical birth and involves a cosmic conception governed by divine laws. It is not a matter of faith or belief in dogma, nor a matter of worship or the reading of scripture. It is realized by employing a system that can be applied by the individual in harmony with God. Therefore, Christ is not a matter of faith but of actual involvement in which the participant communicates with God by means of a divine language.

The oral Gospel has not come down to the Christian Church. For this reason the Christian religion is not complete, for the whole message and purpose of the early Church was to involve humankind in the Kingdom of God. Having been lost for centuries, the Gospel can only be reinstituted by Christ at the Second Coming, at which time the universal message of Christ is to be carried far beyond the Christian world, just as the first message was carried beyond the Hebrew people.

God, who spoke the Word in times past to members of the human family through prophets possessed by the Holy Spirit, elects to send a preexistent being into the world from time to time to instruct humankind. Such was Jesus, then, who was Christ manifest as a man. He came to restore the supernatural knowledge of God to humanity.

Jesus, the Christ, was above the Laws of the Ancient Fathers. Though Jesus possessed a human nature, He also was divine. The man was rejected by His fellows and killed on a tree, a sacrifice not to God but to humanity's own ignorance of a greater Law than that of the scribes and the lawmakers. The words of Jesus inspired a limited following among the Hebrew people, and these inspired ones were sacrificed, one by one, until nothing remained but the memory of their deeds. While He was alive, Jesus spoke the divine words to these disciples, words that were never transcribed onto scrolls. With the death of Jesus and His immediate followers, the secret tradition was preserved among a handful of followers. Such persons were ascetics living in communities away from the metropolitan areas. They cared neither for glory, fame, nor personal achievement, desiring rather to preserve the words and await the command of God. Slowly, the number of those who preserved the words grew smaller and smaller until nothing remained but their writings: selected scrolls intended as guides for order within their own communities or for inspiration as the Holy Spirit filled them. These writings were shrouded in cryptic symbology, allegory, and parables and thus were encoded in such a manner as to render them useless except to those who possessed the means to decode them. It was from these writings and fragments of the oral tradition that the later writings came into being, forming the tracts and letters that compose the New Testament. Still others form the Apocrypha and other noncanonical writings that have survived over the centuries. In this manner the Christian Church came into being, eventually assuming the Authoritative or Popular Church. The Word of God became secondary to Law or Dogma, and again the Spirit of the Word was lost to the Churches as it had been before in ancient times.

The prophets spoke of the apostasy that would engulf the Church and promised that Christ would come again in the latter days, inspiring people and regenerating the Church for a Second Advent and a greater glory than ever before.

That the early Christian communities were isolated and the teachings secret can be established by the fact that there is hardly any mention of the Church in the writings of the historians of that time. Josephus, the Jewish historian who wrote of the Essenes, knew nothing of Jesus and His teachings. Justus of Tiberias, born in Galilee about the time of the crucifixion, does not mention Jesus. Philo, a mystic and philosopher of Alexandria who lived and wrote during the first fifty years of Christianity, does not have a single reference to Jesus in any of his numerous works. Responsible scholars who have sought to reconstruct the life and works of Jesus have given up in despair, aware that the origins of Christianity are not to be traced to the man called Jesus. The popular notion that Christianity, following the death of Jesus, inflamed the Roman world into a spiritual state is not borne out by historians. The Church did not begin to spread until after the last half of the first century CE. Christianity became popular around the second century and did not triumph until the fourth century, when Emperor Constantine made it the state religion.

What was the secret tradition that was guarded so jealously by the immediate disciples of Jesus and that seems to have died with them? How is it to be repossessed if it is not preserved in the Gospels or Church tradition?

It certainly cannot be repossessed by interpretation of the existing writings of the New Testament. Qualified scholars have attempted to do so before, but such attempts have only tended to spotlight the inadequacy of the writings and the existence of numerous interpolations, mutilations, dislocations, and alterations placed in later copies by unauthorized compilers who worked from earlier manuscripts now no longer extant. Our so-called authoritative copies are not identical with the original manuscripts. Indeed, we only have copies of copies that were altered over the centuries.

The problem began early. Jesus and His disciples spoke Aramaic. His immediate followers did not write down what He said. Much later, when the oral traditions preserved by the faithful were put into writing, the larger part was written in Hebrew and the parts that survived were recopied in the *koine* (common) Greek spoken in the greater Mediterranean area. Most copies were done on the cheaper papyrus, which tended to disintegrate due to the humid climate. The fragments that survived were recopied on more permanent vellum and parchment. Not until the late fourth century CE was a complete copy of the Bible compiled from available sources, including that of the great library of Pamphilus. This copy was a Latin translation of the Hebrew, done by Eusebius Hieronymus (better known as Saint Jerome) and became known as the Vulgate, or commonly used version, which became the approved Bible of the Roman Catholic Church. However, this Church established itself as the sole source of the infallibility of Christian doctrine and repressed all further translations into vernacular languages. Jerome judged what should be included in the New Testament canon; namely, the four Gospels, Acts, the fourteen epistles of Paul of the first order, and accepted the Book of Revelation with some reservation (the latter had been excluded in earlier canons, the oldest known such list being from the so-called Muratorian Fragment, which was compiled late in the second century at Rome). A number of books, later declared heretical, were also accepted. Some were used for church services, others only for private readings: James, Jude, 2 Peter, 2 and 3 John.

All other works were rejected and considered spurious—a rather large number of secret or hidden works that Jerome did not understand and thus rejected. Pope Leo I (the Great) also considered these writings forbidden and in the fourth century ordered them burned. In view of these burnings and rejections, vast numbers of valuable scrolls, fragments, and books that could have shed light upon early Christianity were lost forever. Christians who came later were thus denied meaningful documents that could have informed them of the traditions of the early Church Fathers. Modern scholars have been forced to confine their studies to the canonical Bible (which was determined by the Council of Laodicea in 363 CE, the third Council of Carthage in 397), and again, much later, by the Council of Trent in 1546 in response to the Protestant Reformation), portions of scripture preserved among the Eastern Churches, and others that have come to light in recent years.

Although theologians and some biblical scholars have declared that none of the Apocrypha or Pseudepigrapha writings has been unjustly excluded from the New Testament, by implying that the apocryphal Gospels, acts, epistles, testaments, revelations, and other so-called false or spurious works are not up to the standards of the canonical, or accepted, writings, they cannot be certain of this because so much has been lost. Moreover, some of the Pseudepigrapha, written in the first two centuries before the birth of Jesus, were used by the Essenes and early Christians, though later excluded by the established Christian Church. The messages of these writings is cryptic. Secret symbols were inserted by the compilers, for which the reader required keys to interpret. These were given only during a long initiation period.

Later Christians and biblical compilers, being uninformed of this tradition, rejected the writings as false and misleading; therefore, in the case of Jerome, who took it upon himself to be the sole judge of what was to be included in the canon, molded Christianity to his own ends. Whether this was well intended or not is beside the point. The fact remains that what came to be accepted as the Christian scriptures was selected, edited, and classified not by Jesus or His immediate disciples, nor even by those who lived in the first century, but rather by persons living centuries later who had not had the benefit of the original manuscripts, much less the oral teachings known only to the earliest Christians. This rejection of the hidden teachings by the ecclesiastics of the age indicates that the teachings indeed had been encoded by the ancient writers with cryptic symbology and were not understood by the later examiners. Without the keys given to the early initiates, the works took on the appearance of confused allegory and were thus labeled false and taken out of circulation. Eventually, they were forbidden for public reading and even private reading and soon became lost for all time.

We begin to see that the secret oral teachings and the cryptographic scrolls held in trust by the original communities, founded by Jesus and the disciples, were forgotten or lost and were later replaced by formalized dogma. In other words, the Church ceased to be a secret order and became a public institution. This began to take place in the latter half of the first century when the primitive Palestine community spread into the great cities of the Roman Empire. It had its beginnings with Paul, who adapted the teachings he had learned to the mentality of the Gentile masses. The change spread further with the death of Peter and the leaders of the Palestine churches and reached a climax with the destruction of Jerusalem under the Roman general Titus in 70 CE.

The establishment of a New Kingdom of God on earth beginning with Israel, as envisioned by Jesus, was never achieved. Later, the builders of the Church at Rome sought to create a popular religion with organized worship that would satisfy the varied needs of the masses spread throughout the Roman Empire, as opposed to a mystical order composed of master teachers inspired by Christ. The small Christian Community, with its antisocial teachings, which had disturbed both the Roman and Jewish leaders, was replaced by foreign members who took over leadership and altered the teachings. The change became complete when Christianity was established as the state religion under Constantine early in the fourth century. With the fall of the Roman Empire in 476 CE, followed by the Dark Ages, whatever hope remained of repossessing the early traditions as preserved by oral tradition or original manuscripts was lost.

Since the original and authentic teachings of Jesus disappeared long before the creation of the popular Church outside of Palestine, it can safely be said that the Christian Church can in no way lay claim to the tradition. The oral teachings that seem to have been lost centuries before the establishment of the organized Church were in no way preserved by the order that followed.

The New Testament writings, including those outside the canon, equally have not preserved the tradition. The Gospels were catechisms intended for the instruction of Christian initiates. They were not an account of Jesus describing His character, life, and teachings. The earliest books, written a generation after His death, were allegorical, and the teachers possessed the keys to their explanation. Once the initiates were admitted into the community and entrusted with the oral teachings, the penalty for putting them to the printed word as received was instant death at the hand of God. The legitimate teachings of Jesus, then, are not to be found in the New Testament. Left only with the catechisms, scholars and theologians have been baffled as to the genuine teachings of Jesus. It becomes increasingly clear that the early Christians possessed a secret tradition that never came down to the popular Church to this day.

Be this as it may, surviving Christian scripture does contain inherent truths that may be reclaimed through proper interpretation. To accomplish this we must move into a new dimension of interpretation, away from the literal meaning, even beyond the allegorical, apocalyptic, ecclesiastical, theological, or topological interpretations common to biblical exegesis.

Interpretation of the Bible was as much of a problem to the Jews as it was later to Christians. The Jewish tradition gave birth to the Pharisees, who taught that the Torah had both a written and an oral doctrine. The Pharisees could be traced back as early as Ezra. They gradually gained popular support because they interpreted the Word of God as being meant for the entire nation, carrying the Law into the average home. Their influence radiated from the synagogue and encompassed the popular masses, for they attempted to uplift the people to the level of priests, in keeping with the commandments of God. Their ranks included priests, members of the aristocracy, and the scribes who became the copyists, interpreters, and guardians of the Law. Formalists, legalists, and democrats, they incurred the wrath of Jesus and His disciples, and later that of Paul, because their oral traditions, passed along from trained rabbis to scholastic pupils, were overly complicated and became dogmatic practices. Their forerunners may have been the Hassideans (Hasidim) during Maccabean times. On the other hand, there were the Sadducees: the wealthy, educated, and aristocratic minority stemming from the Maccabean dynasty, who opposed the Pharisees on the grounds that the Law of Moses must be applied to the letter. They were the custodians and the guardians of ancient scripture, who rejected the oral traditions of the elders and carried on a common tradition that was shared by other peoples, including the Greeks and Romans. Then there were the Zealots, nationalists who preached against the Sadducees and like the Pharisees, defended the exclusiveness of Judaism against all other peoples and religions. Their center was Galilee, and their fiery revolt against Rome cost many Jewish lives. The city of Sepphoris, a Zealot stronghold near Nazareth, was attacked by Roman legions, who hung the rebels on a forest of crosses in the nearby hills. Jesus might very well have been influenced by these events, which occurred during His youth.

Jesus was unsympathetic toward the scribes and Sadducees. Being from the north, He was probably familiar with the Zadokite priesthood, many of whom later associated with the Gnostic ideas and who were identified with the Sadducees and the Essene groups around the Dead Sea. They did not recognize Jerusalem and Mt. Zion as the proper place for the sanctuary of God. This explains why the Dositheans from this area went on to be influenced by Gnostic thought. Jesus was well versed in the Pentateuch, Torah and the Targums, and He disagreed with the Jewish priesthood at Jerusalem. The Gospels show this clearly. John has Jesus saying to the Jews:

> *Search the scriptures, for in them ye think ye have eternal life: and they are they which testify of me.*
>
> *And ye will not come to me, that ye might have life.*
>
> *I receive not honour from men.*
>
> *But I know you, that ye have not the love of God in you.*
>
> *I am come in my Father's name, and ye receive me not: if another shall come in his own name, him ye will receive.*
>
> *How can ye believe, which receive honour one of another, and seek not the honour that cometh from God only?*

Do not think that I will accuse you to the Father: there is one that accuseth you, even Moses in whom ye trust.

For had ye believed Moses, ye would have believed me; for he wrote of me. But if ye believe not his writings, how shall ye believe my words? (John 5:39–46)

The Jews were hostile toward Jesus, saying to Him: *Say we not well that thou art a Samaritan, and hast a devil?* Galileans, and especially Samaritans, were looked down upon by Judeans. The scriptures told of no prophet coming out of Galilee and thus they would not accept him. To be sure, they were astonished at the words of Jesus, for He spoke with authority that exceeded that of scripture:

Woe unto you, scribes and Pharisees, hypocrites! for ye shut up the kingdom of heaven against men: for ye neither go in yourselves, neither suffer ye them that are entering to go in. Verily, verily I say unto you, He that heareth my word, and believeth on him that sent me, hath everlasting life, and shall not come into condemnation; but is passed from death unto life. . . . For as the Father hath life in himself; . . . so hath He given him authority to execute judgement also, because he is the Son of Man. . . . I can of mine own self do nothing . . . as I hear, I judge: and my judgement is just; because I seek not mine own will, but the will of the Father which hath sent me.

Jesus also proclaimed: *Ye are from beneath; I am from above: ye are of this world; I am not of this world* and *If a man keep my saying, he shall never taste of death.* And the Jews asked how this was possible, for Abraham and the prophets were dead: *Art thou greater than our father Abraham which is dead and the prophets?* And He answered that He did not honor Himself, that it was His Father that honored Him, the same God that they claimed to be their God, but that He knew God and they did not and that if He said He did not know God He would be a liar like them and that their father Abraham rejoiced at His coming into the world. When they questioned Him about the fact that He was not yet fifty years of age and that it was thus impossible for Abraham, who had lived centuries before, to know Him, Jesus proclaimed His spiritual preexistence by stating simply: *Before Abraham was, I am.* Then the Jews took up stones to cast at Him for blaspheming, but Jesus hid himself, His words ringing in the ears of the priests:

> *O Jerusalem, Jerusalem, thou that killest the prophets, and stonest them which are sent unto thee, how often would I have gathered thy children together, even as a hen gathereth her chickens under her wings, and ye would not! Behold, your house is left unto you desolate. For I say unto you, Ye shall not see me henceforth, till ye shall say, Blessed is he that cometh in the name of the Lord.*

The Essenes, like the Pharisees and the Sadducees, had emerged about the time of the decline of the Maccabees, who had claimed kinship with the Spartans. This would account for their mystic tradition, which in many ways had much in common with Hellenic, Egyptian, Zoroastrian, and Mithraic doctrines. The healers or Holy Ones, as they were called in the Aramaic and Greek, refrained from worshipping in the Temple and offering animal sacrifices, though they sent offerings of incense, flour, and oil, and taught that the only true sacrifice to God was a reverent mind. For this reason they believed themselves to be the true Israel. They avoided the cities and the Temple and elected to participate in their sacred rites in the wilderness areas.

The Essenes believed in the immortality of the human soul but not in bodily resurrection. They communed with God facing the sun, as opposed to facing the Temple, as did Jews in the days of Solomon, whose Temple had been oriented to the sunrise, greeting the sun at dawn. An hour before noon they dressed in white vestments and partook of a baptismal act of purification in sacred waters. They had a knowledge of medicine and healed the poor freely, abstaining from all unholy gain, for they had taken an oath never to act unjustly toward other people but to show mercy, to assist the needy, and to live according to natural law. They reverenced God, avoided the wicked, and took an oath to communicate the doctrine of the sect to initiates only as they had received it, and they swore to preserve the anagogical interpretation of certain books and scriptures and to keep the symbols and names of Angels secret. Theirs was a life of justice; holiness; piety; loyalty; saintliness; acceptance of authority, law and order; the knowledge of what is good and bad; love of God, kindness, humanity; and participation in collective fellowship with God through the community as sons of Light.

Another Jewish sect was the Therapeutae (Greek for healers or attendants) who were a sect of the Essenes. They settled around Lake Mareotis near Alexandria, Egypt. They prayed facing the sun at dawn, hands held up to heaven, imploring God to send them brilliant days so that their minds might be illuminated by the Light of truth. They were citizens of heaven and the cosmos who believed in individual salvation as attained through their spiritual exercises during the day, which included a reading of holy scripture. They rejected the literal translation of the scriptures, believing that only through an understanding of the hidden nature of scripture could they understand the true meaning of God's Word. They possessed books of the Old Testament, the Prophets, Psalms, Hymns, Commentaries, and certain secret scrolls written by the founders of the sect that explained the methods of interpreting the inner teachings through their own wisdom, which they sought to develop. After the day's contemplation they again faced the sun at eventide, prayed to God, and then returned to their sanctuaries. As members of the community, the men and women no longer belonged to the world. They lived apart from the national life and the national law, seeking to generate closer union with God. Although both the Essenes and the Therapeutae were influenced by doctrines that appeared to be outside the Judaism of the Pharisees and Sadducees, they were nevertheless representative of an inner and secret Judaism preserved for the elect.

The Christian Community was in existence before the writings of the New Testament came into being. To accept the New Testament as the foundation of Christianity is an error. Quite the reverse is true. Christianity was first preached in Palestine, then spread to the major cities of the Graeco-Roman world. The oral teachings came first, then came letters, sermons, and commentaries. Later came the writings of Paul, and much later still, the Gospels and the Acts, among other writings. It was not until centuries after the death of Jesus and the Apostles that the New Testament as we know it came into existence. And even these writings are compilations from earlier manuscripts since lost to us.

We can conclude then that the New Testament was not the original source of Christianity any more than the Old Testament was the source of Judaism. Something came before it; namely, the oral tradition as spoken by the prophets, which had not come down in the literal translation of scripture. In spite of this, the Bible has become the authoritative holy scripture of both Christian and Jew. We have seen how interpretation of scripture accounted for different sects in Judaism. This has continued into the modern age with the Orthodox, Conservative, and Reform sects, three distinct branches of Judaism. Christendom boasts three main branches: Eastern Orthodox, Roman Catholic, and Protestant, the latter consisting of several hundred denominations, all claiming to possess the proper interpretation of scripture.

The original teachings were always set apart from scripture. They cannot be recovered through a literal translation of the Old Testament scriptures, as the Essenes and Therapeutae said they could not. The same applies to our New Testament writings. There is a hidden truth in Christian scripture that can only be deciphered by anagogical exegesis.

If there is a hidden meaning to scripture, how do we in modern times reclaim the oral tradition that created it? Evidently this tradition is not something to be realized through a scholarly interpretation of scripture, as we have indicated earlier. It can only be realized through some form of divine inspiration given by the very forces that brought the original teachings into existence.

If the original teachings were recovered, they would not only regenerate Christianity but would undoubtedly also be accompanied by supplemental revelations and amendments to our existing scripture. This would represent the Second Advent of Christ to the Christian Community. Indeed, it would amend all existing religions, restoring what has been lost through the ages: The one, true religion that has existed from the beginning. Repossession of this knowledge would extend to all humankind a system of individual salvation through natural and supernatural law in union with God.

We must not concern ourselves with a scholarly interpretation of scripture. We must not seek to explain the cryptic parables or to put words into the mouths of the prophets. A new, human version is not enough. What is needed is the repossession of the living Gospel, given at the command of God through another Christ. This is what every Christian has waited for since the passing of Jesus.

3: THE LOSS OF THE LIVING GOSPEL

Let us now begin to look for traces of the original teaching in Christian scripture so that we may discern for ourselves that it existed for the builders of Christianity not as a dogma or static form of worship but as an actual living system that taught the individual how to attain fellowship with God.

The teachings of the Essenes and Therapeutae were echoed by the community of the faithful at Jerusalem. The baptism of water initiated by John the Baptist was representative of the Essene rite through which an initiate passed in order to participate in the inner teachings. The ritual of washing away of sins was far less important than the spiritual regeneration of the individual as attained through the higher teachings. The relationship between the Essenes and Christianity is indeed impressive. The communal meal, a ritual shared by both, is related, though there are significant differences if we accept a literal reading of the New Testament writings. The Therapeutae held a general assembly every fifty days, after completion of seven sets of seven days; the number seven and its square. This meal was called the *Pannuches* or "all-night" banquet and was related to the Mosaic feast of the wave-loaves in which two loaves and seven lambs were offered to the Lord the first day after the passing of seven Sabbaths—that is, on the fiftieth day—in the feasts of Jehovah.

At sunset the Therapeutae assembled clad in white raiment, hands heavenward, addressing prayers to the sun. Afterward they sat down at table and prayed to God that their meal would be acceptable. Holy scripture was discussed at length, and the president instructed those present on the symbolic meaning of the texts discussed. After this they sang a hymn to God, which was followed by a simple meal of bread and water. They chanted hymns all night until dawn, at which time they went to await the rising sun.

We can see a symbolic relationship between the banquet of the Therapeutae and the feeding of the four thousand in the wilderness, as recounted in the Gospel of Matthew 15:32–37 and again in the Gospel of Mark 8:1–9. Jesus broke seven loaves of bread and gave them to His disciples to set before the people with several small fishes. And when the crowd had finished eating, they took up what was left, which filled seven baskets. This is an allegorical teaching, not to be taken literally, that indicates a common meal consisting of bread and fish that involved the sequence of seven times seven. This banquet has its parallel in the Day of Pentecost, the feast of weeks which took place fifty days after the resurrection (Acts 2:1).

Seven was a sacred number among the Jews, as it was among all ancient peoples, and is mentioned often in both the Old and New Testaments. God's bond with Israel had been concluded on seven occasions: beginning with Noah and the rainbow of seven colors; with Abraham in circumcision; with Moses in the Sabbath of the seventh day; with the Two Tablets of the Ten Commandments; with the Passover; with the Covenant of

Salt; and with the Covenant of the Priesthood of Phineas. The pseudepigraphic Testament of Abraham and the Book of Jubilees foretell of a regeneration of the world after seven millennia and is also outlined in the Qumran text of *The War of the Sons of Light and the Sons of Darkness*, and in the New Testament Gospel of Matthew 24:5–12. God's Light was destined to shine sevenfold strong. The *Book of Hymns*, which is part of the *Manual of Discipline* found among the Dead Sea Scrolls (vol. 7), exemplifies the use of the number seven, in this case applying it to the spiritual regeneration of the individual:

> *I am lit with light sevenfold, with the same lustre of glory which Thou didst create for Thyself. For Thou art unto me as a light eternal keeping my feet upon the way.*

The Talmud also records that in the final days the Messianic sun will be seven times as powerful as normal.

The use of the number seven is again detected in the allegory of the feeding of the five thousand as recorded in the Gospel of Matthew, 14:15–20; the Gospel of Mark, 6:32–43; the Gospel of Luke, 9:10–17; and the Gospel of John, 6:1–13. Here five loaves and two fishes, totaling seven, were used. The fragments left over in this instance filled not seven but twelve baskets. It was eventide and Jesus is said to have looked up to heaven facing the setting sun, blessed the bread, broke it, and gave it to His disciples to give to the multitude. The association with the sun is unmistakable: this event reminds us of the Pannuches meal where the Therapeutae gathered at sunset, stretching their hands to heaven and addressing prayers to God through the sun before partaking of the communal meal. The fragments that filled twelve baskets symbolize the Bread of Life, or the Word of God, distributed to humanity through the rays of the sun. Jesus explains the mystery following the feeding of the five thousand in the Gospel of John, 6:1–66. The reader will find the full text below in the section on the New Testament, but for now, we quote the meaningful lines here:

> *Our fathers did eat manna in the desert; as it is written, He gave them bread from heaven to eat.*
>
> *Then Jesus said unto them, Verily, verily, I say unto you, Moses gave you not that bread from heaven; but my Father giveth you the true bread from heaven.*
>
> *For the bread of God is he which cometh down from heaven, and giveth life unto the world.*

This passage draws its inspiration from Exodus 9:14–36 where the wandering Jews are fed on Manna, a flour-like substance sent down from God, from which the people made wafers of bread.

This represents one of the great mysteries in Christian allegory. The answer can be found in certain Pythagorean elements found in Essenism. The simplest right triangle has sides of 3, 4, and 5 units of measurement. The sum of these units yields the number 12 (3 + 4 + 5 = 12). The sum of the squares of the numbers yields 50 ($3^2 + 4^2 + 5^2$ [or 9 + 16 + 25] = 50). Twelve represented the zodiacal cycle among the Essenes. But the pentecontad cycle, which was based on 50, was higher than the zodiac cycle because the second power of a number is more advanced than the first. The Mishmarot, or Courses, manuscript, found at Qumran on the Dead Sea, describes the rotation, geared to the solar calendar, of the services of the priests. Other manuscripts give the signs of the Zodiac. The Qumran community, undoubtedly related to the Essenes, was ruled by twelve laymen. Jesus appointed twelve Apostles. Just as solar ritual played an important part in the religion of the Essenes and Therapeutae, it was also involved in early Christianity, long before the name *Christian* was applied to the followers of Jesus.

We have pointed out that to the Therapeutae, the number 50 was significant: It was the day following the completion of seven sets of seven days (the squares of the numbers plus the one day equals 50). In manuscripts found in the caves near Qumran there is a reference to *nun*, the fourteenth letter of the Hebrew alphabet, which was assigned the numerological value 50. It is also interesting to note that *nun* in Aramaic is related to the word for "fish", a sign of the universal soul among Semitic peoples.

The Christian sacrament of Communion was instituted by Jesus at the Last Supper when He gathered at eventide with His twelve disciples. The Gospels of Mark, Matthew, and Luke record the event. We quote here from Mark (14:22–26), for brevity's sake:

And as they did eat, Jesus took bread, and blessed, and brake it, and gave to them, and said, Take, eat: this is my body.

And he took the cup, and when he had given thanks, he gave it to them: and they all drank of it.

And he said unto them, This is my blood of the new testament, which is shed for many.

Verily I say unto you, I will drink no more of the fruit of the vine, until that day that I drink it new in the kingdom of God.

And when they had sung an hymn, they went out into the mount of Olives.

We are not told exactly what Jesus said, because the Gospels were not compiled until much later (anywhere from twenty to a hundred years after the death of Jesus), but from what is written, we can see that Mark shows the Paschal character of the Supper—that is, the Jewish Passover commemorating the sacrifice of unblemished lambs by the Jews prior to their exodus from Egypt. The meal consisted of a *eucharistia*, a thanksgiving and a blessing over the wine, lamb, herbs, and unleavened bread. We shall omit the details of the event and move on to the particulars of interest to us here. The Last Supper resembles the Pannuches meal rite of the Therapeutae more than it does the Passover meal. The Eucharist and the transubstantiation, mentioned in the Gospels, where the bread and wine became the blood of the testament, have their parallel in the sacred meals of Attis and Mithra, where the initiate drank blood to establish a mystical union with the blood of the god. Often the blood was symbolized by bread eaten in common brotherhood. Other times the body of a sacrificed animal, such as the bull in Mithraism, was consumed, thereby establishing a bond between the initiate and the divine creature. Paul, knowing of these meals, warns Christians against them in 1 Corinthians 10:20. Paul writes of the importance of the Eucharistic blood in the Christian communion in 1 Corinthians 10:16–17:

> *The cup of blessing which we bless, is it not the communion of the blood of Christ? The bread which we break, is it not the communion of the body of Christ?*
>
> *For we being many are one bread, and one body: for we are all partakers of that one bread.*

Are we to literally accept the text that says it is necessary for Christians to consume the bread and wine, which become the body and blood of Christ? Is this the spiritual process that brings individual salvation, redemption, and illumination? If this is the case, we have nothing more than a syncretism in which Christianity has absorbed a pagan ritual replacing the body of a mythical god or god-animal with that of Jesus, who becomes the atoning sacrifice. It is doubtful that intelligent Jews would have accepted such a teaching. Or is the text of Paul merely a symbolism, a higher teaching with a hidden gnosis? Let us examine 1 Corinthians 11:27–30:

Wherefore whosoever shall eat this bread, and drink this cup of the Lord, unworthily, shall be guilty of the body and blood of the Lord.

But let a man examine himself, and so let him eat of that bread, and drink of that cup.

For he that eateth and drinketh unworthily, eateth and drinketh damnation to himself, not discerning the Lord's body.

For this cause many are weak and sickly among you, and many sleep.

The Jewish Passover is a memorial to the time the people of Israel were spared the destroyer who killed the first-born of the Egyptians when every Israelite household took a male lamb without blemish and bled it. The blood was placed on the two side posts and the lintel of each house. While the occupants ate the flesh and unleavened bread for seven days, they in no way consumed the blood, for this was forbidden to them. Blood was used as a sin offering for atonement to the Lord (Exodus 12:1–15).

No animal sacrificed by the Jews as an atonement was legitimate if it was not killed in the proper place and manner (Leviticus 17:1-9). Blood was forbidden to the Jews under penalty of death:

And whatsoever man there be of the house of Israel, or of the strangers that sojourn among you, that eateth any manner of blood: I will even set my face against that soul that eateth blood, and will cut him off from among his people. For the life of the flesh is in the blood: and I have given it to you upon the altar to make an atonement for your souls: for it is the blood that maketh an atonement for the soul. Therefore I said unto the children of Israel, No soul of you shall eat blood, neither shall any stranger that sojourneth among you eat blood. And whatsoever man there be of the children of Israel, or of the strangers that sojourn

> *among you, which hunteth and catcheth any beast or fowl that may be eaten; he shall even pour out the blood thereof and cover it with dust. For it is the life of all flesh; the blood of it is for the life thereof: therefore I said unto the children of Israel, Ye shall eat the blood of no manner of flesh: for the life of all flesh is the blood thereof: whosoever eateth it shall be cut off.* (Leviticus 17:10–14)

We can see from the writings of the Pentateuch that among the Jews the mere thought of consuming blood was an abomination, unclean, and to be avoided. No teaching that embraced the ceremonial consumption of blood could possibly be accepted. It was forbidden. The idea of Jesus's being a sinless, perfect and worthy sacrifice to atone for humanity's sins would have been inconceivable among the Jews. No bruised or cut animal was worthy of being sacrificed to the Lord (Leviticus 22:24). Jesus was bruised, bleeding from thorns and cut by the lance of a soldier. This fact in itself made the sacrifice unacceptable.

Moreover, any sin-sacrifice had to be killed in the same place as the burnt offering would be made (Leviticus 6:1–30). And the flesh of the sin-offering had to be eaten by the priest in the holy place of the tabernacle of the congregation. But the blood of the sacrifice sprinkled upon any garment was condemned by law to be washed with water. Jesus was killed on Calvary, in the field, and not upon the altar.

We can see from the evidence that the whole idea of Jesus's being a sin-sacrifice is psychologically unacceptable to a Jew. This fact is compounded by the nature of the Jewish mind. Human sacrifice was forbidden. The suggestion that a person had to consume human flesh, even ceremoniously, was something that no Jew could accept. Indeed, Jesus could have been stoned to death according to the Law. That the people often took up stones to throw at him because of His teaching is certain. But to ask

His own disciples to participate in a form of cannibalism and to drink His blood (even ceremoniously) would have been asking too much.

We do not believe that Jesus asked such a thing from God-loving men who had preserved the Law of Moses down through the centuries. To think such a thing is to diminish the stature of the Jews as an intelligent and reasoning people. Knowing how the Jews felt about blood, it is difficult to imagine such a writer as John asking fellow Jews to participate in a Communion of Blood, as a sacrament, to honor Jesus.

Yet, John in the sixth chapter of his Gospel has Jesus say:

Verily, verily, I say unto you, He that believeth on me hath everlasting life.

I am that bread of life.

Your fathers did eat manna in the wilderness, and are dead.

This is the bread which cometh down from heaven, that a man may eat thereof, and not die.

I am the living bread which came down from heaven: if any man eat of this bread, he shall live forever and the bread that I will give is my flesh, which I will give for the life of the world.

The Jews therefore strove among themselves, saying, How can this man give us his flesh to eat?

Then Jesus said unto them, Verily, verily, I say unto you, Except ye eat the flesh of the Son of man, and drink his blood, ye have no life in you.

Whoso eateth my flesh, and drinketh my blood, hath eternal life; and I will raise him up at the last day.

> *For my flesh is meat indeed, and my blood is drink indeed.*
>
> *He that eateth my flesh, and drinketh my blood, dwelleth in me, and I in him.*
>
> *As the living Father hath sent me, and I live by the Father: so he that eateth me, even he shall live by me.*
>
> *This is that bread which came down from heaven: not as your fathers did eat manna, and are dead: he that eateth of this bread shall live forever.* (John 6:47-58)

These were hard words to understand and not spoken in secret among His disciples but in the synagogue in Capernaum. Knowing what we do about the Jews and the restrictions on drinking blood, such a teaching as this spoken in a synagogue would have more than likely resulted in the stoning to death of Jesus.

Indeed John records that several of His disciples did leave Him after this, adding that Jesus, upon seeing that He had offended some of His disciples, qualified His saying by explaining: *It is the spirit that quickeneth; the flesh profiteth nothing: the words that I speak unto you, they are spirit, and they are life* (John 6:63).

We know that Jesus came to fulfill the Law, not to destroy it. Therefore his words are not intended to be taken literally. They are allegorical and have a hidden meaning which was known only to the early Christians after their initiation.

Paul speaks of something far beyond the mere presence of Christ in the bread and wine. It is not simply a spiritual communion but also an act that involves the communicants' psycho-physical attributes. How can the mere taking of bread and wine affect the spiritually prepared one way and the unprepared another way? How can one be made physically weak or sick or even suffer death by the simple act of consuming the Eucharist? There is more involved here than a mere communal meal of bread and wine where Christ is present in the Eucharist. Here is one of the principal mysteries of Pauline thought that represents a hidden knowledge, or gnosis, that was part of Paul's cryptic symbolism. Since the institution of Communion, millions upon millions have shared daily in the sacred ritual for centuries. A large number, perhaps the greater portion, are in many ways unworthy of the transubstantiated bread and wine. Yet they do not grow weak or ill or die.

Did the Communion of Paul's day differ from that of our own? Was there something involved of which the established Churches are ignorant? It would appear so from the testimony that has been given.

We are told that the Essenes, or more specifically the Therapeutae, participated in some form of solar ritual; one in which the aspirant faced the sun at certain times of the day. They took great pains to prepare themselves, living a dedicated life away from the world and giving themselves over to spiritual contemplation and discipline. Was there a hidden reason for this? There is every reason to believe that there was.

The fusion of the individual with cosmic-solar forces was a spiritual art among the ancients. Each sought to absorb through some secret method the energies of the universe into his or her own being—a marriage of the divine with the human. Accumulated energy was to be used for the attainment of a heightened state of being and an expanded sense of reality.

A prolonged period of oral instruction was necessary before the initiate was admitted into such mysteries. Moral discipline, ethical codes of conduct, fellowship, dedication, and obedience were necessary in order for the individual to bring about a union with the Holy Spirit. The initiates were sons and daughters of Light. They did not worship the sun but absorbed the creative energy of the solar forces into their own beings for the overall good of the community and the universe.

The initiates were animated by the rising sun, their minds illuminated by the Light and their spirits joined with God. Their disciplines included the knowledge of cosmic law inherited from the founders of their Orders. Above all, they learned how to commune with the divine will through natural forces.

The uninitiated could in no way participate in these exercises and secret techniques, which were only transmitted orally from teacher to pupil within the confines of the community and over a period of many years. The system remained the property of the communities themselves. Paul's sudden blindness on the road to Damascus, when he experienced a vision at midday under a dazzling light from heaven, exemplifies how an unworthy individual might suffer when facing the Light of God. Paul had persecuted the Christians relentlessly and had journeyed to Damascus, threatening to slaughter the disciples of Jesus. When he saw a vision of Christ appear in the sun, Paul was struck blind and did not regain his sight until three days later after he had repented and pledged to teach Christ to the Gentiles. Afterwards he became a self-proclaimed Apostle.

Can we draw some insight from Paul's experience that might be applied to the matter of the Eucharist? In 1 Corinthians 10:16 Paul writes:

> *The cup of blessing which we bless, is it not the communion of the blood of Christ?*
>
> *The bread which we break, is it not the communion of the body of Christ?*

But later in the same letter (15:35–54), he says quite another thing:

But some men will say, How are the dead raised up? and with what body do they come?

Thou fool, that which thou sowest is not quickened, except it die:

And that which thou sowest, thou sowest not that body that shall be, but bare grain, it may chance of wheat, or of some other grain:

But God giveth it a body as it hath pleased him, and to every seed his own body.

All flesh is not the same flesh: but there is one kind of flesh of men, another flesh of beasts, another of fishes, and another of birds.

There are also celestial bodies, and bodies terrestrial: but the glory of the celestial is one, and the glory of the terrestrial is another.

There is one glory of the sun, and another glory of the moon, and another glory of the stars: for one star differeth from another star in glory.

So also is the resurrection of the dead. It is sown in corruption; it is raised in incorruption:

It is sown in dishonour; it is raised in glory: it is sown in weakness; it is raised in power:

It is sown a natural body; it is raised a spiritual body. There is a natural body, and there is a spiritual body.

And so it is written, The first man Adam was made a living soul; the last Adam was made a quickening spirit.

Howbeit that was not first which is spiritual, but that which is natural; and afterward that which is spiritual.

The first man is of the earth, earthy: the second man is the Lord from heaven.

As is the earthy, such are they also that are earthy: and as is the heavenly, such are they also that are heavenly.

And as we have borne the image of the earthy, we shall also bear the image of the heavenly.

Now this I say, brethren, that flesh and blood cannot inherit the kingdom of God; neither doth corruption inherit incorruption.

Behold, I shew you a mystery; We shall not all sleep, but we shall all be changed,

In a moment, in the twinkling of an eye, at the last trump: for the trumpet shall sound, and the dead shall be raised incorruptible, and we shall be changed.

For this corruptible must put on incorruption, and this mortal must put on immortality.

So when this corruptible shall have put on incorruption, and this mortal shall have put on immortality, then shall be brought to pass the saying that is written, Death is swallowed up in victory.

Here Paul speaks of a spiritual resurrection in which the physical body is of no consequence, and flesh and blood cannot inherit the kingdom of heaven (verse 50). It is apparent, therefore, that the body and blood of Christ in the Eucharist is symbolic of something else.

4: THE WORD: THE IMAGE OF GOD

The Word becomes very clear and precise once the individual is exposed to the real teaching of Christianity: that which Jesus, and especially the Apostles, taught orally and in a hidden way, as well as through the teachings that came down to us in the form of the Gospels, epistles, and in other writings not included in the New Testament canon. It is this hidden message, or Word, that makes Jesus and the Apostles stand out in a glorious and illuminating way when compared to the orthodox and literal translations of the writings.

That the rudiments of this teaching were known prior to the appearance of Jesus is unquestionable. They were preserved by certain sects within Judaism; namely, by the Essenes and Therapeutae. They were also known and preserved among the Greeks, Persians, Egyptians, Romans, Indians, Chaldeans, Babylonians, Chinese, Mexicans, Peruvians, and other great civilizations, many of which we lack knowledge of, but we can suspect included the Britons, French, Germans, Norse, and many, many others that go back far into time before written history. Our knowledge of this teaching is lacking because the later teachings which stem from the original doctrines were altered by persons who, by design or ignorance, changed the original intent of the teachings into human-made concepts that degenerated into organized worship, dogma, and material institutions.

The Christian religion was brought to life by a divine spark generated into existence by God. It sought to restore what was lost to the human family through time. Jesus and the Apostles, therefore, were part of a cosmic plan that emanated out of the Godhead.

That Jesus was a cosmic figure, a preexistent Being come from on high, is beyond question. His immediate disciples, those who came to be known as the Apostles, were inspired by the force of Jesus and the cosmic events that accompanied His appearance; namely, solar and stellar phenomena that always accompany a great Being of Light come to Earth.

Christianity was unique in its time, inasmuch as it was divinely inspired. It was this inspiration that set it apart from the other religions of the time, some of which had been divinely inspired but had decayed into earthly cults called pagan by the early Christians.

The plan of God to instruct humanity in the true life is a process that has been going on since the beginning of humankind. This effort, undertaken by inspired messengers of God, always results in the establishment of a great world religion that eventually decays as the inspiring force is withdrawn for some reason.

The force called Christ, the mediator between humanity and God, was a concept known to many great minds before the advent of Christianity. But mere knowledge of Christ does not bring about its appearance or guarantee humankind's access to it. Christianity, in the beginning, was instrumental in leading humankind back to God through this mediating force.

While various cultures, or groups within these cultures, such as the Essenes or Therapeutae, but not specifically limited to them, sought to preserve the tradition in its purity, they always awaited the next agent of God, whom the Hebrews called the Messiah, the Anointed. To the Qumran sect on the Dead Sea, who carried on the living traditions, believing itself to be the remnant that was to be redeemed, the Messiah was known as the Right Teacher or the Master of Justice, who would establish a greater fulfillment of the teachings they preserved and, they hoped, bring about the end of the age and initiate a new one where God's elect, the People of the Covenant, would have:

> *Everlasting blessings, eternal rejoicing in the victorious life of eternity, and a crown of glory, together with a raiment of majesty in eternal light. (Manual of Discipline, 4:7–8)*

Above all, the Just Teacher, or Teacher of Righteousness, as he has come to be known, would expand upon the divine teaching as revealed to Moses and which the faithful sects preserved against those who had perverted it by literal translation and interpolations. The Anointed One would be a spiritual king of Aaron and Israel who would gather the elect from the four quarters of the world.

The Jerusalem Church under Peter and the other disciples of Jesus, and later the Gentile Community under Paul, reflect many of the ideas of the Essenes, Therapeutae, and the Qumran Community. James, the brother of Jesus, who was called the Just or Righteous One, a pillar of the Church at Jerusalem, expresses the relationship in his writings, as do Peter, John, and Paul. To them there is no question about whether Jesus was the Anointed One, the Right Teacher or Master of Justice. The failure of Israel to accept Jesus as such and their rejection of His message led to the downfall of Israel as a nation at the hands of the Romans.

The Christian and Essene communities all perished later as well, which resulted in the final loss of the teachings.

John has Jesus say: *I am the Light of the world: he that followeth me shall not walk in darkness, but shall have the light of life.* And again: *While ye have light, believe in the light, that ye may be the children of light* (John 8:12; 12:36).

When writing of John the Baptist, John says of him: *There was a man sent from God, whose name was John. The same came for a witness, to bear witness of the Light, that all men through him might believe. He was not that Light, but was sent to bear witness of that Light. That was the true Light, which lighteth every man that cometh into the world* (John 1:6–9). As a messenger, John the Baptist preached: *I am the voice of one crying in the wilderness.* And emulating the discipline of one redeemed: *Make straight the way of the Lord* (John 1:23). John, an Essene, prepared the way of the Right Teacher, the Interpreter of the Law, the Mediator between humankind and God who would baptize not with water but with the Holy Spirit and with fire.

James writes: *Blessed is the man that endureth temptation: for when he is tried, he shall receive the crown of life, which the Lord hath promised to them that love him.* And again: *every good gift and every perfect gift is from above, and cometh down from the Father of Lights* (James 1:12, 17).

From the Dead Sea Scrolls *Book of Hymns*, chapter 4: *I give thanks unto Thee, O Lord, for Thou has illuminated my face with the Light of Thy Covenant, Day by Day I seek Thee, and ever Thou shinest upon me bright as the perfect dawn.* And from the "Hymn of the Initiates" from the *Manual of Discipline*: *For He from the wellspring of Knowledge has made His light to burst forth, and mine eye has gazed upon His wonders, and the light that is in my heart has pierced the deep things of existence.*

Elsewhere in the New Testament are ideas, expressed in the Dead Sea Scrolls, which indicate that the Jewish Christian Church in Jerusalem was an outgrowth of Essene ideas carefully guarded from the days of Moses; for example, that man has two spirits, one dark and the other light, is evident from both Essene and Christian scriptures.

In the Gospel of John, 3:17–21, we read:

> *For God sent not his Son into the world to condemn the world; but that the world through him might be saved.*
>
> *He that believeth on him is not condemned: but he that believeth not is condemned already, because he hath not believed in the name of the only begotten Son of God.*
>
> *And this is the condemnation, that light is come into the world, and men loved darkness rather than light, because their deeds were evil.*
>
> *For every one that doeth evil hateth the light, neither cometh to the light, lest his deeds should be reproved.*
>
> *But he that doeth truth cometh to the light, that his deeds may be made manifest, that they are wrought in God.*

We read in the Community Rule of Qumran:

> *He has created man to govern the world and has appointed for him two spirits in which to walk until the time of His visitation: the spirits of truth and falsehood. All the children of righteousness are ruled by the Prince of Light and walk in the ways of light; but all the children of falsehood are ruled by the Angel of Darkness and walk in the ways of darkness.*

The Epistle of Barnabas, 18:1, states:

> *There are two ways of teaching and of authority, one of light and one of darkness. And there is a great difference between the two ways. For over one are set light-bearing angels of God, but over the other, angels of Satan. And the one is Lord from eternity and to eternity, but the other is prince of the present time of lawlessness.*

Jesus, then, was the long-awaited Right Teacher who interpreted the divine teachings. His appearance restored and fulfilled the religion of the Hebrews as preserved by them. He was condemned by those who should have been the first to accept Him. The letter of the Law had become more important in the formalized worship of the day than the spirit of the Law. The ancient prophets were revered out of all proportion; they were confined to a period of history held sacred. The Messiah was awaited with hope. When He did appear He was rejected because His authority and authenticity were questioned. The Jews expected an earthly king who would forever free them from bondage and oppression, which had begun with the Egyptians and continued under the Babylonians, Greeks, and Romans. The freedom that Jesus offered was of a spiritual kind that would restore God's rule on earth, overthrowing the Powers of Darkness who opposed the Powers of Light and had won over the hearts of most of humanity.

What followed instead was the death of a Great Teacher and shortly thereafter the devastation of Jerusalem and the Jewish state. Instead of a Golden Age that would see the scattered hosts of Israel gathered together under a divine theocracy, they were dispersed. Yet, like a dying star that finally explodes and sends its light forth into the whole universe, the great tradition that had flowered in Israel under Jesus spread to all parts of the world through the Apostles. And the Light of their teachings illuminated the spirits of people everywhere.

The story is repeating itself. The Christian Church of today is under apostasy, bound to the letter of the Law as were the Jews. Christ has become a mere historic figure, confined to the past, revered and worshiped, oftentimes in the form of images of plaster, wood, and stone—something that was violently opposed by the Jews and would have been abhorred by Jesus and His disciples. The new world that God had promised through the prophets had failed to dawn. Thus Christians await—as they have been for nearly 2,000 years—the return of a flesh-and-blood Jesus who will descend from the sky to establish a material kingdom on earth. Like the Jews before them, involved with the letter and dogma of the Law, and looking forward to the establishment of an earthly kingdom by Jesus, their Messiah, Christians have forgotten the spirit of Christ and the spiritual message.

How is it possible for such a learned people as the Jews, sworn to the service of God, and for Christians formed out of the many great civilizations of former ages, to misunderstand so completely the writings of the prophets inspired by God and as interpreted by holy teachers? Above all, how could they fail to grasp the nature of the Right Teacher, and later that of His teachings? The answers lie in the two spirits of humankind—one light, the other dark. It is a basic tenet of Judaism and of Christianity that these two spirits exist. If they exist, then we must acknowledge them and the opposing supernatural powers that work on and through them.

Our references to the Old Testament are based on the fact that the New Testament writings, as well as the Christian teachings, are intimately bound up with it, because Jesus and His teachings were based on a tradition preserved through Jewish history. It must be remembered, however, that when one mentions Hebrew tradition or Old Testament writings, one must include the many schools of thought that were formed by their interpretation of scripture.

Here we come to the original point we are trying to establish: Jesus represented a teaching that was unique and different from the established teachings as interpreted by the Pharisees and Sadducees. Jesus was more representative of the mystic teachings preserved by the Essenes. Indeed, His was a universal teaching: something that was greater than scripture, as is indicated by His authority, which was from God, not scripture. He referred to scripture often in an attempt to show that His concepts were known to the ancient prophets and that He was in harmony with their spiritual message. He was the Messiah, come to fulfill the Hebrew religion, to bring about the Reign of God in a greater way than any imagined—a Reign that the prophets had long predicted. Though His teaching was given to the Jews, it was a universal message that was destined to spread beyond the borders of Israel to all parts of the world. The fact that it spread out from Israel does not necessarily mean that the Gentiles, who formed the Christian Church, understood the message any better than did the Jews.

Jesus was above the Law and the writings of the prophets of the Hebrew religion; just as the spirit of Christ is above the Law and the writings of the Christian religion. The New Testament was born out of Christianity, not Christianity out of the New Testament. The same can be said of Judaism in relation to the Old Testament. It was the Spirit of God that motivated and inspired the prophets. Their interpretation of what God revealed was colored by their human nature. It is the Spirit behind the word that is divine, not the written word itself. That is why John wrote in his Gospel: *In the beginning was the Word, and the Word was with God, and the Word was God. The same was in the beginning with God. All things were made by him; and without him was not anything made that was made. In him was life; and the life was the light of men. And the light shineth in darkness; and the darkness comprehended it not* (1:1–5). To John, Christ was the revealing

Word, the Logos or divine Mediator, who communicated God's Reason to humankind in Light as He had in the beginning, when humans first had life from God.

The early followers of Jesus were Jews who believed in Holy Scripture but, above all, in the true interpretation of it. They accepted Jesus as the Messiah, or Christ, as mediator between God and humankind come to fulfill their religion. In the beginning, the teaching was a fulfillment of Judaism, not a separate formal religion. The separation came later, when the teachings were exported to other peoples.

Therefore, we wish to make clear that we are not attempting a literal interpretation of the Old Testament, nor even of the varied contents of the New Testament, but rather a decoding of the New Testament writings in the true spirit of the Word as divinely revealed and in union with Christ in order to rediscover the message of the living Gospel.

The Gospel writers spoke of Jesus as baptizing with the Holy Spirit and with fire. What was meant by this statement? Is there some relationship with the very special and supernatural communion referred to by Paul?

We have some hint in the words of John where he speaks of the bread that comes down from heaven and that those who eat of it shall never die but shall live forever. We have here a symbolism of some hidden teaching that is not made clear in the New Testament, at least not from a literal point of view. We are forced to look outside the canonical writings for some understanding.

In 64 CE, the Christian communities at Rome were either killed or scattered; both Peter and Paul were dead. The Church at Jerusalem, as well as that at Rome, ceased to exist. What remained was a handful of Christians who had been initiated into the mysteries. There was no authoritative body, and there were no master teachers. Only the oral traditions and some fragments of early writings survived. For all intents and purposes, the Community that had been envisioned by Jesus and the disciples perished as surely as if it had been crucified on the cross along with Jesus.

The Roman general Titus destroyed the Temple and put to death a large number of Christians and Jews. Under the new emperor, Titus's father, Vespasian, Christians were forbidden to practice their religion. During the first two centuries, different forms of Christianity and various churches developed. In 303 CE all Christian sacred scrolls were ordered destroyed by Emperor Diocletian. Thus, valuable fragments, scrolls, and manuscripts were lost forever. Slowly, the Roman Church absorbed what remained, and when Christianity became the official state religion, all books that were not authorized—that is, those deemed heretical—were burned. Churches that opposed the setting of the New Testament canon were persecuted.

Christian scripture has had a long and troubled history. Most of the books in our present New Testament were known at a reasonably early date. That they have existed for so many centuries without being destroyed makes them highly suspect, Scholars, even those unschooled in the inner teachings, are aware of the many adulterations, alterations, interpolations, and inconsistencies in the writings. The Christian who wants to get at the genuine message of Christ must look beyond the so-called authoritative Christian scriptures. As we have said, Christianity did not develop out of the New Testament.

Nevertheless, scripture does contain a great amount of truth and knowledge when it is interpreted in an anagogical, or higher, spiritual, manner. It would also be an error for any interpretation to impose a system foreign to what was preached by Jesus. In view of this, any modern interpretation could only come from the expressed authority of Christ. The reader must also be aware that any interpretation of scripture must be based on the oral teachings given to the ordained and that are not put to the printed word in their entirety, as has been traditional with the sacred Christology.

To understand the symbolic terms used by the inspired writers, we must examine parts of apocryphal and pseudepigraphic writings that were used by early Christians, and in some cases by the Essene or Qumran sects in Palestine, who, as we know, possessed the hidden keys to their understanding but which were rejected by the later organized Church and left out of the Bible. This indicates two schools of thought: the formalized one of the later organized Church, and the mystical one founded by Jesus. Therefore, the reader must accept that although the organized Christian Church—that is, Catholic Christianity—claims guardianship over the traditions and teachings of Jesus and the Apostles, it certainly was not founded by Jesus, Paul, or Peter. Catholic Christianity, like Protestant Christianity, came at a much later date and was man-made.

The claim that Jesus founded the Church on Peter, not God, has absolutely no grounds when examined by the enlightened reader. The Gospel of Matthew (16:16–18) has Peter reply to Jesus's question to the disciples about His identity: *And Simon Peter answered and said, Thou art the Christ, the Son of the living God. And Jesus answered and said unto him, Blessed art thou, Simon Barjona: for flesh and blood hath not revealed it unto thee, but my Father which is in heaven. And I say also unto thee, That thou art Peter, and upon this rock I will build my church.* That the Church was to be built upon God, the rock, and not Peter the man, is evident from the following quote from the New Testament's First Letter of Peter:

> *As newborn babes, desire the sincere milk of the word, that ye may grow thereby:*
>
> *If so be ye have tasted that the Lord is gracious.*
>
> *To whom coming, as unto a living stone, disallowed indeed of men, but chosen of God, and precious,*
>
> *Ye also, as lively stones, are built up a spiritual house, an holy priesthood, to offer up spiritual sacrifices, acceptable to God by Jesus Christ.*
>
> *Wherefore also it is contained in the scripture, Behold, I lay in Sion a chief corner stone, elect, precious: and he that believeth on him shall not be confounded.*
>
> *Unto you therefore which believe he is precious: but unto them which be disobedient, the stone which the builders disallowed, the same is made the head of the corner,*
>
> *And a stone of stumbling, and a rock of offence, even to them which stumble at the word, being disobedient: whereunto also they were appointed.*
>
> *But ye are a chosen generation, a royal priesthood, an holy nation, a peculiar people; that ye should shew forth the praises of him who bath called you out of darkness into his marvellous light. (2:2–9)*

We see this idea expressed in the Community Rule of the Dead Sea Scrolls:

> *He that is everlasting is the support of my right hand. My footpath is over stout rock which nothing shall shake, for the rock upon which I walk is the truth of God and His might is the support of my right hand.*

And again in the *Book of Hymns* from the Dead Sea Scrolls:

I give thanks unto Thee, O my God,

I extol Thee, O my Rock.

Jesus is quoted in the Gospel of Matthew as saying in His famous Sermon on the Mount:

Therefore whosoever heareth these sayings of mine, and doeth them, I will liken him unto a wise man, which built his house upon a rock.

And the rain descended, and the floods came, and the winds blew, and beat upon that house; and it fell not: for it was founded upon a rock.

And every one that heareth these sayings of mine, and doeth them not, shall be likened unto a foolish man, which built his house upon the sand:

And the rain descended, and the floods came, and the winds blew, and beat upon that house; and it fell: and great was the fall of it.

And it came to pass, when Jesus had ended these sayings, the people were astonished at his doctrine:

For he taught them as one having authority, and not as the scribes. (7:24–29)

5: MYSTERY OF THE DIVINE NOURISHMENT

There was an incredible difference between the formalized state religion at Rome and the living Gospel that represented the genuine teachings of Jesus. Those teachings, which differed from the accepted doctrines established by Catholic Christianity and to which the word *heretical* or *spurious* was applied, were only heretical in the sense that they did not comply with the canonical or literal interpretation of New Testament writings and the doctrines formulated by the later Church.

It seems incredible that the Rome that destroyed the Temple at Jerusalem and dispersed the Jews and that killed Jesus and the Apostles and tens of thousands of Christians eventually went on to establish itself as the sole authority over the teachings of Jesus and the Jewish Apostles. This incredibility is emphasized when we see how the teachings were absorbed and altered from the original form, the sources of which were burned by imperial decree.

This situation is compounded by the Protestant Churches, which grew and developed out of the older Roman Church and interpreted the New Testament and Old Testament in a most literal manner. These churches were as ignorant of the original teachings as was the Church of Rome, thus perpetuating the tradition begun in the first and second centuries. This tradition sprang from minds who were ignorant of the true teachings and accepted the literal translation of the New Testament writings. Not having been initiated into the mysteries, they did not understand that God had spread His Light over the world, as revealed by Jesus, and they did not know the proper method of sustaining the new-age force, much less how to instruct others in it. As a result, the Messianic Age dimmed and finally died. The Gospel of Thomas records: *His disciples said to Him: On what day will the Kingdom come?* Jesus answered: *It will not come by expectation; they will not say: See, here, or: See, there. But the Kingdom of the Father is spread out on the earth and men do not see it.* Jesus makes clear that the Kingdom *is* something that exists and people must be made to see it through a proper interpreter of the divine teachings. By so doing, humankind is able to participate in the redeeming force of God's grace and help bring about the establishment of a new Earth under God. In other words, God is not going to suddenly change the world. Humankind must alter its own situation by its own efforts with the help of God. This is the meaning of Christ as a saving force sent by God.

That humankind has been kept ignorant of this truth by the very forces supposedly ordained to perpetuate it bespeaks of the evil Powers of Darkness bent on keeping the human family from the knowledge of God as taught by those sent from the abodes of Light. This is not to say that the Christian Churches freely choose to keep the laity ignorant of God's truth and knowledge. They are as ignorant of the higher teachings of Christianity as those they seek to serve. The evil was done ages ago by a power greater than humanity; the same power that crucified Jesus, killed the Apostles and the early Christians, destroyed the Temple and

Jerusalem, hunted down the Guardians of the Sacred Teachings of Light, defiled the teachings, usurped the power of the Fathers, and established instead a teaching that did not glorify the Light or the Cross of Enlightenment, the Word made manifest, but instead put Jesus on the tree, saying that the shedding of His blood was for the atonement of humanity's sins. The pagan rituals were continued—the very rituals that Jesus sought to do away with. The Apostles and the first Christians in Israel would have abhorred such concepts.

In the very beginning, Christian instruction was given orally. Later, this instruction was copied down, encoded, and put into a flowery symbology as was common among the mystery schools of the day. When the original manuscripts were recopied, the copyists, ignorant of the true meaning, used a literal language. None of the original manuscripts written by Paul and other early writers are extant. Only copies of copies remain. The manuscripts used by Mark, Matthew, and Luke are missing as well as varied sources such as the Logia (sayings), Q (another sayings source), and the so-called Urmarcus (an earlier version of the Gospel of Mark). We know that the writers of the Synoptic Gospels were working with collected teachings from the masters as committed to memory by their disciples and later to scrolls that were by no means complete. To a large degree the Synoptic Gospels are artificial and filled with interpolations. Thus the writings of the New Testament that were known in Rome as early as 200 CE, and accepted as authoritative in 367 CE, were no less corrupted than our own. The alterations began at a very early date.

For this reason we must seek the true wisdom of the writings through some means other than a superficial examination of scripture. The wisdom can only be discovered by means of divine inspiration from the power responsible for bringing them into existence: Christ.

To continue to confuse the symbolic sayings attributed to Jesus and the disciples with fact and history would lead to eventual degeneration of the Christian Consciousness and the loss of the great eternal message. With such a collapse, Christianity would degenerate to the level in which the pagan religions found themselves at the appearance of Jesus in the ancient world.

The words of the Qumran Community Rule guide us:

> *For my light has sprung from the source of His knowledge; my eyes have beheld His marvellous deeds, and the light of my heart, the mystery to come. From the source of His righteousness is my justification, and from His marvellous mysteries is the light in my heart. My eyes have gazed upon what is eternal, on wisdom concealed from men; on knowledge and wise design hidden from the sons of men, on a fountain of righteousness, on a storehouse of power, on a spring of glory hidden from the assembly of flesh. God has given them to His chosen ones as an everlasting possession, and has caused them to inherit, the lot of the Holy Ones. He has joined their assembly to the Sons of Heaven, to be a Council of the Community, a foundation of the Building of Holiness, an everlasting Plant throughout all ages to come.*

And the Hymns scroll assures us that the interpretation of divine scripture suffered corruption from earliest times:

> *Teachers of lies have smoothed Thy people with words, and false prophets have led them astray; they perish without understanding for their works are in folly. For I am despised by them, and they have no esteem for me that Thou mayest manifest Thy might through me. They have banished me from my land like a bird from its nest. . . . All my friends and brethren are driven far from me and hold me for a broken vessel.*

> *Teachers of lies and seers of falsehood, they have schemed against me a devilish scheme, to exchange the Law engraved on my heart*

by Thee for the smooth things which they speak to Thy people.

The Gospel of Philip has Jesus saying:

The Pharisees and the Scribes took the keys of knowledge; they hid them. They did not enter, and they did not allow to enter those who wanted to enter.

To better understand the symbolic terms used by Paul and John, we should first examine the apocrypha and pseudepigrapha not included in the canon of the New Testament. We refer first to the Gospel of Philip, contained in the sacred writings of the Gnostic Christians of Egypt and Syria. These selections shed some light upon the mysteries of the second birth that comes from water and the spirit and also of the Eucharist:

We are born through the Holy Spirit, but we are born again through the Christ. In both we are anointed through the Spirit. When we were born we were united.

No one can see himself in water or in a mirror without light.

Nor again will you be able to see in light without water or a mirror. On account of this it is fitting to baptize in both the light and the water. But the light is the Anointing.

There were three buildings for offering-places in Jerusalem. One was open to the west; they called it "the holy." Another was open to the south; they called it "the holy of the holy." The third was open to the east [the sun door] ; they called it "the holy of the holies." It was the place into which the high priest came alone. The Baptism is the holy house. the holy of the holy. The holy of the holies is the Bridal-chamber. Baptism has the resurrection and the Salvation in order to hasten into the Bridal-chamber. But the Bridal-chamber is in that which is greater than. . . [This portion of the text is missing, but the importance of the Bridal-chamber is stressed. We see from the next passage that the souls of men and women are restrained by the powers, but that the Light put on in the Bridal-chamber is superior to the powers that seek to harm mankind].

The powers cannot see those who put on the perfect light, and they cannot hold them. But one will put on the light in the Mystery, in the joining.

If it is fitting, I will speak a mystery: the Father of All joined himself with the Virgin who came down, and a light surrounded him that day. He revealed the great Bridal-chamber. Therefore, his body came into being that day. He came out of the Bridal-chamber as one who came into being from the bridegroom and the bride. Thus, Jesus established the All through these. And it is fitting for each of his disciples to enter his repose.

In this world the slaves serve the free. In the Kingdom of Heaven, those who are free will serve the slaves. The children of the Bridal-chamber will serve the children of the marriage. The children of the Bridal-chamber have a name . . . the repose . . . them. They do not need. . . . [text missing].

Those who say 'They will die first and rise again' are in error. If they do not first receive the resurrection while they live, when they die they will receive nothing. So also they speak about Baptism, saying that Baptism is a great thing, because if people receive it they will live. The apostle Philip said: Joseph, the carpenter, planted a garden because he needed the wood for his craft. He made the Cross from the trees which he planted. And his seed hung on what he had planted. His seed was Jesus, but the planting was the Cross" [The Tree of Life].

The Anointing is greater than Baptism. For by the Anointing we are called "Christians," not because of Baptism. And they call Christ so because of the Anointing. For the Father anointed the Son, and the Son anointed the apostles, and the apostles anointed us. He who has been anointed has the All; he has the resurrection, the Light, the Cross, the Holy Spirit. The Father gave him these things in the Bridal-chamber; he received.

The Cup of Prayer holds wine, it holds water. It serves as a type of the blood by which they give thanks [the eucharist]. And it is full of the Holy Spirit and it belongs to the completely perfect Man. When we drink this, we will take to ourselves the perfect Man. The living water is a body. It is fitting that we clothe ourselves with the living Man. Therefore, when he comes to go down to the water, he disrobes in order that he may put this one on.

A horse begets a horse; a man begets a man; a God begets a God. It is thus with the bridegroom and the bride.

The holy man is all holy, including his body. For, if he holds the bread, he will make it holy, or the cup, or anything else which he holds, he will make it pure. And how is it he will not make the body pure?

He who has the knowledge of the truth is free. But the free man does not sin. For he who sins is the slave of sin. The Mother is the truth. The knowledge is the Father. To whomever it is given not to sin, the knowledge of the truth lifts up the heart, that is, it makes them free and raises them over the whole earth. Love, however, builds up. And he who has become free through the knowledge is a slave on account of love to those who cannot yet take the freedom of knowledge.

The Logos said: "If you know the truth, the truth will make you free. Ignorance is a slave. Knowledge is freedom. If we know the truth we will find the fruits of the truth in us. If we join with it, it will bring the fullness of God to us."

We now have the revealed things of creation. We say: "They are the worthwhile, strong things. But the hidden things are worthless and weak." Thus it is with the revealed things of the truth; they are weak and worthless. But the hidden things are strong and worthwhile. However, the mysteries of the truth are revealed as types and images. But the Bridal-chamber is hidden. It is the holy one in the holy one.

The veil at first covered how God administered the creation. But when the veil is torn, and the things within are revealed, it will leave this house as a desert; rather, it will be void. But the whole divinity will not flee out of these places back into the holies of holies. For it cannot mix with the pure light and the faultless fullness of God, but it will be under the wings of the Cross and under its arms. This ark will be used for their escape when the deluge of water overpowers them. If some are in the tribe of the priesthood, they will be able to enter behind the veil with the high priest. Because of this the veil was not torn only on top, because it would be open only for those above. Nor was it torn only at the bottom, since it would be revealed only to those below. Rather, it was torn from the top to the bottom. Those of above opened to us of below; therefore, we will go into the secret of truth. This truly is the worthwhile which is strong. But we will go in there through worthless types and weaknesses. They are really worthless in respect to the perfect glory. There is a glory which is greater than glory. There is a power greater than power. Therefore, this has opened the perfect to us, and the secret of the truth. And the holy ones of the holy ones are revealed, and the Bridal-chamber urged us in. As long as it is hidden, the wickedness is really made nothing, but it is not removed from the midst of the seed of the Holy Spirit. They are slaves of evil. When it is revealed, then the perfect light will pour over all and all in it will receive the Anointings. Then the slaves will become free and the prisoners will be redeemed. Every plant my Father in Heaven does not plant will be rooted out. Those who are alienated will be united. Everyone who will go in to the Bridal-

chamber will be born of light. For they are not conceived from the marriage which is consecrated in the night. The fire of the flesh burns in the night; but afterwards it is extinguished. But the mysteries of marriage are fulfilled in the day and light. That day or its light does not set.

If anyone becomes a child of the Bridal-chamber, he will receive light. If anyone does not receive it while he is in these places, the world, he will not be able to receive it in the other place. The one who has received light can not be seen nor can he be held, and no one can torment him, even if he lives in the world. And also, if he should go out of the world, already he has received the truth in images. The world became the aeon, for the aeon is become for him the fullness of God, and it is thus: it is revealed only to him. It is not hidden in the darkness and the night, but it is hidden in a perfect day and a holy light.

These beautiful but cryptic lines seem to agree with the words of Jesus, who speaks about a second birth when a person would be born of water and the spirit. The Gnostic sectarians point out the importance of the Holy of Holies situated in the Temple facing the east, where the sun rises and the new birth takes place. Baptism is a prerequisite to the anointing that takes place when one puts on the Light. In the Gnostic writings the emphasis is on the Tree of Life, the cross of knowledge, the Light, and the resurrection rather than on the tree on which Jesus hung. The mystery of the Eucharist is explained: the cup of prayer holds wine and water, serving as a *type* of blood (that is, symbolical), but the new birth in the Bridal-chamber is realized by the Light of Christ.

The Gospel of Philip also hints at the Light of God shed upon the earth and how the Light Spirit of humans responds to it while the Dark Spirit of humans is not able to understand it:

> *A blind man and one who can see, if they are in the dark there is no difference between them. When the light comes, then the one who sees will see the light, and the one who is blind will stay in the darkness. . . . There is light within a man of light and it lights the whole world. When it does not shine, there is darkness.*

Paramount in the teachings of the Gnostic Christians was the doctrine that the Elect of God are in reality trapped in the world of Darkness, but that once they are awakened by the Light of Christ they are freed from the world and restored to the Godhead. That is why the Gospel writer has Jesus saying:

> *Blessed is the one who exists before he comes into being. For he who exists, he was and will be.*

This same idea is expressed in the Gospel of Thomas (49–50) and the Acts of Thomas (15). Thus when the Elect are awakened, they become united in fellowship regardless of race, creed, sex, or color. Philip illustrates the universality of Christ in his Gospel in the following lines:

> *The Lord went into the dye-shop of Levi. He took seventy-two colors: he threw them into the kettle. He took them all out white and he said: "Thus the Son of Man came, a dyer."*

The Christian Church opposed Gnosticism. In Revelation 2:6, John appears to write against the Nicolaitanes, a certain sect of the Gnostics. There was speculation among the Gnostics that the Supreme God of the Universe and the Creator of the World were two separate beings, with the latter an inferior being, because matter was the source of all evil. Further speculation included the concept that there were two natures dwelling in Jesus —the divine nature and the human nature. These were two separate natures: Christ who had descended from God, and the human nature of the man Jesus, united only by the two dwelling together.

Did the writer of the Book of Revelation actually oppose the concept of two indwelling natures in Jesus, or is this line spurious, inserted at a later date by a redactor to comply with some theological dogma? Certainly, this would explain why the Book of Revelation was rejected by many of the early Christian communities. John tells us in his Gospel that the Word was of God and dwelt among us. This bespeaks the divine and human natures of Jesus.

The texts themselves are always secondary to the oral teachings. We cannot participate in the teachings of Christ by a reading of scripture; for Christ's message is a living system to be experienced. The Word of God is not the written word but that which is communicated by God through the Spirit of Christ to the Light of the individual's spirit. It is extremely important for the reader to keep this fact uppermost in his or her mind. Christ is the Supreme Overseer of our understanding of ancient scripture, as well as the Revealer of all new teachings being given in this modern day and age through a New Ministry of the New Advent under Christ as prophesied.

Though this new order comes as a fulfillment of Christianity, it has a universal message. The main purpose of this volume is to explain to the reader the hidden meaning of scripture preserved by the Holy Schools of antiquity in Israel and elsewhere. The early writers wrote for a select group of individuals, formed into communities, who required instruction and weaning from pagan rites that often included blood sacrifice. Therefore, a literal translation of New Testament Scripture must be taken with a grain of salt. Some examples of what we mean are: the emphasis on God come in the flesh; that the world is saved by the blood of the Lord; that the body is resurrected; and similar ideas or expressions that stress the body rather than the spirit.

Verification that the ancient writings cannot serve modern-day Christians is the new Appearance of Christ come to instruct mankind with illuminated teachings for the growth and evolution of the human family in today's world. The bickering that went on in the first and second centuries shows only too clearly that the ancients, including some of the Apostles, were involved in theological dogmatizing. Instead of seeing the beauty of humankind illuminated by the Light of God through the teachings of Christ as given by Jesus, and the making of a new world, they got bogged down in dogma. In the old days the High Priest went alone into the Holy of Holies of the Tabernacle, but not without a blood offering (see Letter to the Hebrews 9:6–7) as a sacrifice to God for the errors of the people. With the coming of Jesus it was taught that He was the blood sacrifice that replaced all other sacrifices and that it was no longer necessary to offer the blood of animals (Hebrews 9:11–13). The offering of blood seemed to be a vital element to the ancients, and the idea has continued down to the present age with the sacrament of communion in which the bread and wine are considered to be transubstantiated into the body and blood of Jesus. This is a continuation of pagan rites and ceremonies, which were perpetuated by simply replacing the animals with Jesus. The Gnostics, who preserved the ancient teachings from Israel, Egypt, and Greece, attempted to emphasize the Light instead of the blood in religious ceremony; individual knowledge over sacrifice; and individual salvation through new birth in the here and now as opposed to something which might take place in the distant future through faith. They were the true Christians who stressed the Light. The neo-Christians wished to carry on the Law and the sacrifices at the Temple, which even the Essenes had refused to acknowledge, because they considered the sacrifices to have been offered to an inferior being and not to the True God.

We can see how the noble teachings of Christ in Jesus were perverted and the pagan beliefs and practices simply continued in another form. It was for this reason that the message of the New Testament writers who stressed the Law of Moses and the blood sacrifice of Jesus appear to be opposed to the Gnostics. We cannot be certain, though we can suspect, that compilers inserted these ideas at a later date to confirm their dogma. There can be no other explanation, considering that so many Gnostic terms are used in the New Testament—the word *Logos* in John being only one of the more important ones. If this is not the case, then the entire message of Jesus was misunderstood.

We do know, however, that the message of Jesus was a spiritual one. John has him say: *It is the spirit that quickeneth; the flesh profiteth nothing: the words that I speak unto you, they are spirit, and they are life* (John 6:63). Blood and flesh have no place in the teachings of Jesus if we consider the meaning of these words. Again John has Him say: *I am the Light of the world; he that followeth me shall not walk in darkness, but shall have the light of life.... If a man keep my saying he shall never see death.... Verily, verily, I say unto you, Before Abraham was, I am* (John 8:12, 51, 58). We see here the Gnostic idea of preexistence in a higher world of Light. These words reflect the ancient wisdom known to many of the Schools of antiquity. They differ in that Jesus addressed the populace with the phrase: *I say unto you,* demonstrating an authority that superseded that of the Law and the Prophets. He taught not from the scripture but from spiritual truths. He announced to individuals a new way to supernatural knowledge through participation in the divine secrets, in fellowship with God, which is not realized by one's own efforts alone but through the redeeming power of the mediating Light called God's grace. That is why John has Jesus say in the sixth chapter of his Gospel:

Then Jesus said unto them, Verily, verily, I say unto you, Except ye eat the flesh of the Son of man, and drink his blood, ye have no life in you.

Whoso eateth my flesh, and drinketh my blood, hath eternal life; and I will raise him up at the last day.

For my flesh is meat indeed, and my blood is drink indeed.

He that eateth my flesh, and drinketh my blood, dwelleth in me, and I in him.

As the living Father hath sent me, and I live by the Father: so he that eateth me, even he shall live by me.

This is that bread which came down from heaven: not as your fathers did eat manna, and are dead: he that eateth of this bread shall live forever.

These things said he in the synagogue, as he taught in Capernaum.

Many therefore of his disciples, when they had heard this, said, This is an hard saying; who can hear it?

When Jesus knew in himself that his disciples murmured at it, he said unto them, Doth this offend you?

What and if ye shall see the Son of man ascend up where he was before?

It is the spirit that quickeneth; the flesh profiteth nothing: the words that I speak unto you, they are spirit, and they are life. (John 6:53-63)

Here Jesus is speaking about His preexistent and present spiritual nature, and of the Light of which He is composed. The blood is strictly symbolic, as is the flesh, and is not to be confused with the blood of His material body, which His spirit or being merely occupies so that He may manifest to man. In other words, His followers must "eat" the Light and the Spirit of Christ in order to gain eternal life—not just the Light, but the Christ within that Light.

The second and third chapters of Genesis contain a symbolism regarding Adam, the First, Perfect Man, made of Light in the image of God, who was forbidden to eat of the Tree of the Knowledge in the Garden. We read:

And the LORD God formed man of the dust of the ground, and breathed into his nostrils the breath of life; and man became a living soul.

And the LORD God planted a garden eastward in Eden; and there he put the man whom he had formed.

And out of the ground made the LORD God to grow every tree that is pleasant to the sight, and good for food; the tree of life also in the midst of the garden, and the tree of knowledge of good and evil. . . .

And the LORD God commanded the man, saying, Of every tree of the garden thou mayest freely eat:

But of the tree of the knowledge of good an evil, thou shalt not eat of it: for in the day that thou eatest thereof thou shalt surely die. . . .

And Adam gave names to all cattle, and to the fowl of the air, and to every beast of the field; but for Adam there was not found an help meet for him,

And the LORD God caused a deep sleep to fall upon Adam, and he slept: and he took one of his ribs, and closed up the flesh instead thereof;

> *And the rib, which the LORD God had taken from man, made he a woman, and brought her unto the man.*

God provided Adam with divine nourishment from the Tree of Life, which gave Adam's brilliant body of Light immortality. But of the Tree of Knowledge of Good and Evil he was forbidden to eat lest he become as a god. Furthermore, God warns Adam that should he eat of the Tree of Knowledge of Good and evil, his nature would become mortal. But Eve, being full of innocence, was tricked by the Dark Angel, Lucifer, into eating of the dual Tree of Knowledge of Good and Evil, and consequently she persuaded Adam to eat its fruit, too. We read from the third chapter of Genesis:

> *Now the serpent was more subtle than any beast of the field which the LORD God had made, And he said unto the woman, Yea, hath God said, Ye shall not eat of every tree of the garden?*
>
> *And the woman said unto the serpent, We may eat of the fruit of the trees of the garden:*
>
> *But of the fruit of the tree which is in the midst of the garden, God hath said, Ye shall not eat of it, neither shall ye touch it, lest ye die,*
>
> *And the serpent said unto the woman, Ye shall not surely die:*
>
> *For God cloth know that in the day ye eat thereof, then your eyes shall be opened, and ye shall be as gods, knowing good and evil,*
>
> *And when the woman saw that the tree was good for food, and that it was pleasant to the eyes, and a tree to be desired to make one wise, she took of the fruit thereof, and did eat, and gave also unto her husband with her; and he did eat,*
>
> *And the eyes of them both were opened.* (Gen. 3:1–7)

Afterwards, God expelled Adam and Eve from the Garden, knowing that they had become full of knowledge of good and evil, like gods, and that if they ate of the Tree of Life they would live forever (filling the universe with even greater knowledge of good and evil). We read in the allegorical story:

> *And the LORD God said, Behold, the man is become as one of us, to know good and evil: and now, lest he put forth his hand, and take also of the tree of life, and eat, and live forever:*
>
> *Therefore the LORD God sent him forth from the garden of Eden, to till the ground from whence he was taken,*
>
> *So he drove out the man; and he placed at the east of the garden of Eden Cherubims, and a flaming sword which turned every way, to keep the way of the tree of life. (Gen. 3:22-24)*

Thus Adam was denied the fruit of the Tree of Life and became mortal. The symbolism of the story is interesting when we understand the meaning of the words.

Cherubim and a flaming sword guarded the Garden of Eden from the east so that Adam and Eve could not gain access to the Tree of Life. The symbolism is very clear: the cherubim were always associated with the Holy of Holies in the Temple, guarding the Sun Door facing the rising sun to the east. Cherubim were usually depicted as winged figures, either with human faces or as bulls, lions or eagles—all solar creatures. In Solomon's Temple, cherubim were made from olive wood, standing ten cubits tall; i.e., about twelve feet high. Olive oil was used in the perpetual flame burning in the Tabernacle. Cherubim were also represented as clouds—the chariots of God. The flaming sword represents our parent or material sun. So we see that the angels and the fire of the sun guarded access to the Tree of Life, which is God's Light—the Primordial Sun of Justice.

The story continues in the first verse of the fourth chapter of Genesis:

> *And Adam knew Eve his wife; and she conceived, and bare Cain, and said, I have gotten a man from the Lord.*

In Gnostic literature, Cain (or Kae) is one of the Angelic Powers representing the sun. The symbolism is quite evident to the reader who has been given the oral and written traditions provided in the Sacred Teachings of Light as part of the New Ministerial Training. The Light of God (the Tree of Life) was the divine nourishment that made the First Man, Adam, immortal in the beginning. The Tree of Knowledge of Good and Evil is a secondary kind of food that nourishes the psychic and physiological processes of the new human created by archetypal Adam and Eve. Our material sun is a source of knowledge, as taught by the Gnostics and other ancient schools of former times, but spiritual man is made immortal not by knowledge, but by God's Light, which gave birth to the material sun.

Paul warns his followers who were taught the Holy Way the dangers involved in eating of the Tree of Life and partaking of the divine food. When Paul told of some of his followers who had become sick and had even died as a result of the process, he meant to make it very clear that there were many dangers involved in the second birth, wherein humans threw off the mortal nature with the conception of the immortal nature. It was essential for these regenerated humans to penetrate the lesser light of the sun in order to gain access to the greater spiritual Light.

John has Jesus saying in the seventh chapter of his Gospel:

> *In the last day, that great day of the feast, Jesus stood and cried, saying, If any man thirst, let him come unto me, and drink.*

> *He that believeth on me, as the scripture hath said, out of his belly shall flow rivers of living water. (John 7:37-38)*

John explains these words in Revelation 22:1–5:

> *And he shewed me a pure river of water of life, clear as crystal, proceeding out of the throne of God and of the Lamb.*
>
> *In the midst of the street of it, and on either side of the river, was there the tree of life, which bare twelve manner of fruits, and yielded her fruit every month: and the leaves of the tree were for the healing of the nations.*
>
> *And there shall be no more curse: but the throne of God and of the Lamb shall be in it; and his servants shall serve him:*
>
> *And they shall see his face; and his name shall be in their foreheads.*
>
> *And there shall be no night there; and they need no candle, neither light of the sun; for the Lord God giveth them light: and they shall reign forever and ever.*

Jesus must have appeared as a madman to the Jews, who were governed by the letter of the Law. No one but a madman could speak so boldly, unless, of course, he was what he claimed to be—a son of God. Again in chapter 7 of his Gospel John has Jesus saying:

> *Now about the midst of the feast Jesus went up into the temple, and taught.*
>
> *And the Jews marvelled, saying, How knoweth this man letters, having never learned?*
>
> *Jesus answered them, and said, My doctrine is not mine, but his that sent me.*

> *If any man will do his will, he shall know of the doctrine, whether it be of God, or whether I speak of myself.* (John 7:14-17)

It becomes apparent that Jesus was a preexistent Being come to earth to teach the human family and announce access to the Tree of Life, which is God, not Himself (something that is made very clear throughout the New Testament). He possessed a certain knowledge of life and the Law. He came to teach the Children of Adam spiritual truths and how to access eternal life through God. As Adam had been created by God, so the Christ nature in Jesus was created by God and dwelled within the human nature of the man Jesus. Jesus was therefore a complex of both divine and human natures.

John has Jesus say: *And now, O Father, glorify thou me with thine own self with the glory which I had with thee before the world was* (John 17:5). This statement indicates the preexistence of Jesus, that He was in fact a Being of Light with God before the world was made. *I am not of the world,* Jesus states from time to time.

Jesus also declares that Moses spoke of His coming, referring to the following prophecy recorded in the Book of Deuteronomy 18:15–19:

> *The LORD thy God will raise up unto thee a Prophet from the midst of thee, of thy brethren, like unto me; unto him ye shall hearken;*
>
> *According to all that thou desiredst of the LORD thy God in Horeb in the day of the assembly, saying, Let me not hear again the voice of the LORD my God, neither let me see this great fire any more, that I die not,*
>
> *And the LORD said unto me, They have well spoken that which they have spoken.*

I will raise them up a Prophet from among their brethren, like unto thee, and will put my words in his mouth; and he shall speak unto them all that I shall command him,

And it shall come to pass, that whosoever will not hearken unto my words which he shall speak in my name, I will require it of him.

With this statement Jesus claims Messiahship and that His appearance in the world was preordained by God and prophesied by Moses, the Lawgiver. The Messiah would be a messenger, not a king, and He would bring new teachings. Thus His authority came from God.

Therefore, Jesus must have believed Himself to be the Messiah, for no prophet could claim such authority. Jesus did not turn His people away from God, only from the letter of the Law as taught by the lawgivers, the scribes and Pharisees. He preached the Kingdom of God, which was above the Law and the prophets (Luke 16:16).

Indeed, Jesus was relentless in His attack upon the lawgivers. We read in Luke 11:45–54:

Then answered one of the lawyers, and said unto him, Master, thus saying thou reproachest us also.

And he said, Woe unto you also, ye lawyers! for ye lade men with burdens grievous to be borne, and ye yourselves touch not the burdens with one of your fingers.

Woe unto you! for ye build the sepulchres of the prophets, and your fathers killed them.

Truly ye bear witness that ye allow the deeds of your fathers: for they indeed killed them, and ye build their sepulchres.

Therefore also said the wisdom of God, I will send them

prophets and apostles, and some of them they shall slay and persecute:

That the blood of all the prophets, which was shed from the foundation of the world, may be required of this generation;

From the blood of Abel unto the blood of Zacharias, which perished between the altar and the temple: verily I say unto you, It shall be required of this generation.

Woe unto you, lawyers! for ye have taken away the key of knowledge: ye entered not in yourselves, and them that were entering in ye hindered.

And as he said these things unto them, the scribes and the Pharisees began to urge him vehemently, and to provoke him to speak of many things:

Laying wait for him, and seeking to catch something out of his mouth, that they might accuse him.

Moses prophesied not only the coming of the Messiah but also of false prophets. In Deuteronomy he wrote: *When a prophet speaketh in the name of the Lord, if the thing follow not, nor come to pass, that is the thing which the Lord hath not spoken, but the prophet hath spoken presumptuously.* Thus the scribes and the Pharisees hoped to trap Jesus into blasphemy and label Him a false prophet. Of course, Jesus committed many acts contrary to the Law. He ate the shewbread, which was not lawful to eat except by the high priests. He healed on the Sabbath. He did not always wash before eating. And there were many other acts for which He was criticized. He constantly emphasized that He was above the Law (which, of course, was contrary to good law and order). He was not a priest with legal authority but self-proclaimed. It was from the northern parts, known as the Galilee, that Jesus came forth, and many of the lawyers argued that the scriptures nowhere stated that a prophet would come from these parts. Galilee was looked down on by Judeans because it was a place of mixed races, the descendants of Babylonians who had settled there during the Captivity, and thus it was now a land of Gentiles. Since He spoke Aramaic, many of the parables and sayings of Jesus were misunderstood by Judeans. Though He performed miracles and healed many, it was Jesus's disassociation from the Law that led to His condemnation by the Jewish authorities and His eventual judicial murder under the authority of the Romans.

6: JESUS PROPHESIES THE SECOND COMING

Jerusalem fell to the Romans in 70 CE, and the people were led captive out of the promised land, forty years following the crucifixion. *Verily I say unto you, There shall not be left here one stone upon another, that shall not be thrown down.* The prophecy of the day of vengeance, recorded in Matthew, was uttered by Jesus during the Olivet Discourse when He predicted the destruction of the Temple.

But, of all the prophecies of Jesus, it was the promise of the Second Coming and the establishment of the Kingdom of God on earth that stirred Christians to action. Luke tells us in his Gospel (17:20–24):

And when he was demanded of the Pharisees, when the kingdom of God should come, he answered them and said, The kingdom of God cometh not with observation:

Neither shall they say, Lo here! or, lo there! for, behold, the kingdom of God is within you.

And he said unto the disciples, The days will come, when ye shall desire to see one of the days of the Son of man, and ye shall not see it.

> *And they shall say to you, See here; or, see there: go not after them, nor follow them.*
>
> *For as the lightning, that lighteneth out of the one part under heaven, shineth unto the other part under heaven; so shall also the Son of man be in his day.*

Matthew records the prophecy in his Gospel (24:27–31):

> *For as the lightning cometh out of the east, and shineth even unto the west; so shall also the coming of the Son of man be,*
>
> *For wheresoever the carcass is, there will the eagles be gathered together,*
>
> *Immediately after the tribulation of those days shall the sun be darkened, and the moon shall not give her light, and the stars shall fall from heaven, and the powers of the heavens shall be shaken:*
>
> *And then shall appear the sign of the Son of man in heaven: and then shall all the tribes of the earth mourn, and they shall see the Son of man coming in the clouds of heaven with power and great glory.*
>
> *And he shall send his angels with a great sound of a trumpet, and they shall gather together his elect from the four winds, from one end of heaven to the other.*

The Gospel writers link the Second Coming with the light that shines out of the east. The Coming is related to the sun rising in the east. John's Revelation (19:17) testifies to this Second Coming and the relation to the light of this new sun, seen in a vision of an angel with a rainbow as a crown and clothed in a cloud:

> *And I saw an angel standing in the sun; and he cried with a loud voice, saying to all the fowls that fly in the midst of heaven, Come and gather yourselves together unto the supper of the great God;*

John's vision continues in chapters 21:22–24:

> *And I saw no temple therein: for the Lord God Almighty and the Lamb are the temple of it.*
>
> *And the city had no need of the sun, neither of the moon, to shine in it: for the glory of God d lighten it, and the Lamb is the light thereof.*
>
> *And the nations of them which are saved shall walk in the light of it: and the kings of the earth do bring their glory and honour into it.*

And again in 22:1–5:

> *And he shewed me a pure river of water of life, clear as crystal, proceeding out of the throne of God and of the Lamb.*
>
> *In the midst of the street of it, and on either side of the river, was there the tree of life, which bare twelve manner of fruits, and yielded her fruit every month: and the leaves of the tree were for the healing of the nations,*
>
> *And there shall be no more curse: but the throne of God and of the Lamb shall be in it; and his servants shall serve him:*
>
> *And they shall see his face; and his name shall be in their foreheads.*
>
> *And there shall be no night there; and they need no candle, neither light of the sun; for the Lord God giveth them light: and they shall reign forever and ever.*

We read here of God's Light, the primordial Sun of God that is to be restored to the world. God's Light is to be nourishment for a Light body and is as different from the material sun as the material body is from the spiritual Light body. This Light from the Tree of Life shall overcome death while giving a new life. We read from Paul's first epistle to the Corinthians (I Cor. 15:20–26):

> *But now is Christ risen from the dead, and become the firstfruits of them that slept.*
>
> *For since by man came death, by man came also the resurrection of the dead.*
>
> *For as in Adam all even so in Christ shall all be made alive.*
>
> *But every man in his own order: Christ the firstfruits; afterward they that are Christ's at his coming,*
>
> *Then cometh the end, when he shall have delivered up the kingdom to God, even the Father; when he shall have put down all rule and all authority and power.*
>
> *For he must reign, till he hath put all enemies under his feet.*
>
> *The last enemy that shall be destroyed is death.*

In verses 35–51 of the same chapter Paul explains the resurrection of the spiritual man who triumphs over death:

> *But some man will say, How are the dead raised up? and with what body do they come?*
>
> *Thou fool, that which thou sowest is not quickened, except it die:*
>
> *And that which thou sowest, thou sowest not that body that shall be, but bare grain, it may chance of wheat, or of some other grain:*
>
> *But God giveth it a body as it hath pleased him, and to every seed his own body.*
>
> *All flesh is not the same flesh: but there is one kind of flesh of*

men, another flesh of beasts, another of fishes, and another of birds.

There are also celestial bodies, and bodies terrestrial: but the glory of the celestial is one, and the glory of the terrestrial is another.

There is one glory of the sun, and another glory of the moon, and another glory of the stars: for one star differeth from another star in glory.

So also is the resurrection of the dead. It is sown in corruption; it is raised in incorruption:

It is sown in dishonour; it is raised in glory: it is sown in weakness; it is raised in power:

It is sown a natural body; it is raised a spiritual body. There is a natural body, and there is a spiritual body.

And so it is written, The first man Adam was made a living soul; the last Adam was made a quickening spirit.

Howbeit that was not first which is spiritual, but that which is natural; and afterward that which is spiritual.

The first man is of the earth, earthy: the second man is the Lord from heaven.

As is the earthy, such are they also that are earthy: and as is the heavenly, such are they also that are heavenly.

And as we have borne the image of the earthy, we shall also bear the image of the heavenly.

Now this I say, brethren, that flesh and blood cannot inherit the kingdom of God; neither doth corruption inherit incorruption.

> *Behold, I shew you a mystery; We shall not all sleep, but we shall all be changed,*

We learn the nature of this new body of Light from Paul's Epistle to the Philippians, where he mentions that his labors are on heavenly things, from whence all men look for the Savior, the Lord Jesus Christ, who will transform the material body to the likeness of His glorious body according to His mighty power, whereby He is able to subdue all things unto Himself.

The apocalyptic teachings that the world would soon come to an end by divine intervention and that God's Kingdom would be established forever were an integral part of the early Christian teaching. This apocalyptic idea stemmed from the earlier Old Testament writings, especially from those preserved and interpreted by the Essenes and related orders, such as the Therapeutae and those of Qumran on the Dead Sea. It was based on the concept of the Two Ways: the Children of Light allied with the Powers of Light and the Children of Darkness allied with the Powers of Darkness. It was generally believed among Christians, as evidenced by their zealous teachings along these lines, that the end of the age was expected to arrive soon.

That the end did not come as expected remains one of the supposed shortcomings of the Christian doctrine. Its failure to materialize does not mean that Jesus and His followers failed in any way or that the prophecy was wrong. The whole concept has been misunderstood from earliest times, owing to the literal translation of the apocalyptic writings, or revelations, by later compilers who did not understand the symbology, consisting of various images, signs, numbers, phrases, and the like, used by the evangelists schooled in the ancient art of spiritual cryptology to encode the writings with hidden meanings in such a way as to render them meaningless except to those initiated into the mysteries. This was a time-honored practice among the sects in the land in which Jesus and the disciples hailed; a practice which later baffled the Roman and Greek redactors who did not speak the ancient Aramaic and thus relied on their own judgment in translating such works for the western mentality.

Mark's Gospel has Jesus coming into Galilee proclaiming the Kingdom of God, saying: *The time is fulfilled, and the kingdom of God is at hand: repent ye* (which, in the Greek of Mark's Gospel was rendered "metanoeite" and means to have a change of heart, to change one's ways) *and believe the gospel* (Mark 1:15).

Jesus was declaring that something greater than the Law had come into the world. He taught that the blessings of a new age were being given by God to restore what had been taken away in the Garden with the fall of Adam and Eve. Matthew has Jesus saying:

> *Think not that I am come to destroy the law, or the prophets: I am not come to destroy, but to fulfil.*
>
> *For verily I say unto you, till heaven and earth pass, one jot or one tittle shall in no wise pass from the law, till all be fulfilled.*
>
> *Whosoever therefore shall break one of these least commandments, and shall teach men so, he shall be called the least in the kingdom of heaven: but whosoever shall do and teach them the same shall be called great in the kingdom of heaven.*
>
> *For I say unto you, That except your righteousness shall exceed the righteousness of the scribes and Pharisees, ye shall in no case enter into the kingdom of heaven.* (Matthew 5:17–20)

Jesus was teaching a New Way. It was within the Law that this Way had come to replace the sin-offering of blood for atonement. There was a new bread—a bread direct from God that extended immortality of the soul. Those living within the new teaching could quite easily live within the letter of the Law while still involving themselves in the spiritual benefits. The Law did not of itself extend immortality, but those sharing in the benefits of God's grace were obligated, as good Jews, to uphold the Law as laid down by the prophets, and by so doing exceed the righteousness of the scribes and Pharisees. The new teaching was one of even greater responsibility, but the adherents of the new doctrine were free to disregard that portion of the Law deemed superfluous, as Jesus and His disciples demonstrated from time to time, much to the chagrin of the lawyers.

The extent of this responsibility is briefly referred to in the Egyptian Gnostic document called Pistis Sophia:

> *The Saviour answered again and said unto Mary: "Amen, amen, I say unto thee: The man who hath known the godhead and hath received the mysteries of the Light, and sinned and hath not turned to repent, he will get suffering in the chastisements of the judgments in great sufferings and judgments exceedingly far more in comparison with the impious and law-breaking man who hath not known the godhead. Now, therefore, who hath ears to hear, let him hear."*

The Apocryphal work known as the General Epistle of Barnabas, written by a fellow preacher with Paul, and hailed by many of the early Church Fathers as a genuine canonical writing and read in the churches of Alexandria, sums up the general feeling among Christians of the day regarding the legal sacrifices and how the spiritual righteousness replaced them. We quote from chapter 2:

> *Seeing then the days are exceeding evil, and the adversary has got the power of this present world we ought to give the more diligence to inquire into the righteous judgments of the Lord.*
>
> *Now the assistants of our faith are fear and patience; our fellow-combatants, long-suffering and continence.*

Whilst these remain pure in what relates unto the Lord, wisdom, and understanding, and science, and knowledge, rejoice together with them.

For God has manifested to us by all the prophets, that he has no occasion for our sacrifices, or burnt-offerings, or oblations: saying thus; To what purpose is the multitude of your sacrifices unto me, saith the Lord.

I am full of the burnt-offerings of rams, and the fat of fed beasts; and I delight not in the blood of bullocks, or of he-goats.

When ye come to appear before me; who hath required this at your hands? Ye shall no more tread my courts.

Bring no more vain oblations, incense is an abomination unto me; your new moons and sabbaths; the calling of assemblies I cannot away with, it is iniquity, even the solemn meeting; your new moons and your appointed feasts my soul hateth.

These things therefore hath God abolished, that the new law of our Lord Jesus Christ, which is without the yoke of any such necessity, might have the spiritual offering of men themselves.

That following the New Way brought about a change in the person is apparent—this was not just a change of personality, a mere alteration of the person's character (though this must have been part of it), but the appearance of a New Person. It was as if the newly made person were enveloped in a Light that shone brilliant and glorious. A new consciousness came forth, and the New Person spoke in heavenly language. This reconstruction of a person was not brought about by faith or belief in new doctrines or by some emotional change due to the presence of Jesus. It was brought about by eating the Bread of Life extended by God that nourished dormant faculties. A new birth did take place, and the regenerated individual took on the qualities of the true nature of

Humanity. This is very apparent as well from the Epistles of Paul quoted in the previous pages.

What was this new bread, the fruit of the Tree of Life, that actually made possible the emergence of a New Person out of the old?

We learn, again from the words of Barnabas (chapter 2), that one did experience a spiritual change through following the New Way that Jesus taught:

> *And when he chose his apostles, which were afterwards to publish his Gospel, he took men who had been very great sinners; that thereby he might plainly shew, That he came not to call the righteous but sinners to repentance.*
>
> *Then he clearly manifested himself to be the Son of God. For had he not come in the flesh, how should men have been able to look upon him, that they might be saved?*
>
> *Seeing if they beheld only the sun, which was the work of his hands, and shall hereafter cease to be, they are not able to endure steadfastly to look against the rays of it.*
>
> *Wherefore the Son of God came in the flesh for this cause, that he might fill up the measure of their iniquity, who have persecuted his prophets unto death. And for the same reason also he suffered.*

But what was the catalyst that brought about this change in the men and women who followed Jesus? And what did it have to do with the figurative language used by the early writers where blood and wine and light are interwoven? We quote again from the apocryphal Pistis Sophia:

> *Jesus said unto his disciples: "Draw near unto me." And they drew near unto him. He turned himself towards the four corners of the world, said the great name over their heads, blessed them and breathed into their eyes.*

Jesus said unto them: "Look up and see what ye may see.

And they raised their eyes and saw a great, exceedingly mighty light, which no man in the world can describe.

He said unto them anew: "Look away out of the light and see what ye may see."

They said: "We see fire, water, wine and blood."

Jesus said unto his disciples: "Amen, I say unto you: I have brought nothing into the world when I came, save this fire, this water, this wine and this blood. I have brought the water and the fire out of the region of the Light of the lights of the Treasury of the Light, and I have brought the wine and the blood out of the region of Barbelo. And after a little while my father sent me the holy spirit in the type of a dove.

"And the fire, the water and the wine are for the purification of all the sins of the world. The blood on the other hand was for a sign unto me because of the human body which I received in the region of Barbelo, the great power of the invisible god. The breath on the other hand advanceth towards all souls and leadeth them unto the region of the Light.

"For this cause have I said unto you: 'I am come to cast fire on the earth,'—that is: I am come to purify the sins of the whole world with fire.

"And for this cause have I said to the Samaritan woman: 'If thou knewest of the gift of God, and who it is who saith unto thee: Give me to drink,—thou wouldst ask, and he would give thee living water, and there would be in thee a spring which welleth up foreverlasting life.'

"And for this cause I took also a cup of wine, blessed it and give it unto you and said: 'This is the blood of the covenant which will be poured out for you for the forgiveness of your sins.'

"And for this cause they have also thrust the spear into my side, and there came forth water and blood.

"And these are the mysteries of the Light which forgive sins; that is to say, these are the namings and the names of the Light."

It came to pass then thereafter that Jesus gave command: "Let all the powers of the Left go to their regions." And Jesus with his disciples remained on the Mount of Galilee. The disciples continued and besought him: "For how long then hast thou not let our sins which we have committed, and our iniquities be forgiven and made us worthy of the kingdom of thy father?"

And Jesus said unto them: "Amen, I say unto you: Not only will I purify your sins, but I will make you worthy of the kingdom of my father. And I will give you the mystery of the forgiveness of sins, in order that to him whom ye shall forgive on earth, it will be forgiven in heaven, and he whom ye shall bind on earth, will be bound in heaven. I will give you the mystery of the kingdom of heaven, in order that ye yourselves may perform the mysteries for men."

And Jesus said unto them: "Bring me fire and divine branches." They brought them unto him. He laid out the offering, and set down two wine-vessels, one on the right and the other on the left of the offering. He disposed the offering before them, and set a cup of water before the wine-vessel on the right and set a cup of wine before the wine-vessel on the left, and laid loaves according to the number of the disciples in the middle between the cups and set a cup of water behind the loaves.

Jesus stood before the offering, set the disciples behind him, all clad with linen garments, and in their hands the cipher of the name of the father of the Treasury of the Light, and he made invocation thus, saying: "*Hear me, O Father, father of all fatherhood, boundless Light: iaō iouō iaō aoi ōia psinōther therōpsin ōpsither nephthomaōth nephiomaōth marachachta marmarachta iēana menaman amanēi israi amēn amēn soubaibai appaap amēn amēn deraarai amēn amēn sasarsartou amēn amēn koukiamin miai amēn amēn iai iai touap amēn amēn amēn main mari mariē marei amēn amēn amēn.*

"*Hear me, O Father, father of all fatherhood. I invoke you yourselves, ye forgivers of sins, ye purifiers of iniquities. Forgive the sins of the souls of these disciples who have followed me, and purify their iniquities and make them worthy to be reckoned with the kingdom of my father, the father of the Treasury of the Light, for they have followed me and have kept my commandments.*

"*Now, therefore, O Father, father of all fatherhood, let the forgivers of sins come, whose names are these: siphirepsnichieu zenei berimou sochabrichēr euthari na nai dieisbalmerich meunipos chirie entair mouthiour smour peuchēr oouschous minionor isochobortha.*

"*Hear me, invoking you, forgive the sins of these souls and blot out their iniquities. Let them be worthy to be reckoned with the kingdom of my father, the father of the Treasury of the Light.*

"*1 know thy great powers and invoke them: auēr bebrō athroni ē oureph ē ōne souphen knitousochreōph mauōnbi mneuōr souōni chōcheteōph clōche eteōph memōch anēmph.*

"*Forgive the sins of these souls, blot out their iniquities which they have knowingly and unknowingly committed, which they have committed in fornication and adultery unto this day;*

forgive them then and make them worthy to be reckoned with the kingdom of my father, so that they are worthy to receive of this offering, holy Father.

"*If thou then, Father, hast heard me and forgiven the sins of these souls and blotted out their iniquities, and hast made them worthy to be reckoned with thy kingdom, mayest thou give me a sign in this offering.*"

And the sign which Jesus had besought happened.

Jesus said unto his disciples: "*Rejoice and exult, for your sins are forgiven and your iniquities blotted out, and ye are reckoned with the kingdom of my father.*"

And when he said this, the disciples rejoiced in great joy.

Jesus said unto them: "*This is the manner and way and this is the mystery which ye are to perform for the men who have faith in you, in whom is no deceit and who hearken unto you in all good words. And their sins and their iniquities will be blotted out up to the day on which ye have performed for them this mystery. But hide this mystery and give it not unto all men, but unto him who shall do all the things which I have said unto you in my commandments.*

"*This then is the mystery in truth of the baptism for those whose sins are forgiven and whose iniquities are blotted out. This is the baptism of the first offering which showeth the way to the region of Truth and to the region of the Light.*"

Thereafter his disciples said unto him: "*Rabbi, reveal unto us the mystery of the Light of thy father, since we heard thee say: 'There is still a fire-baptism and there is still a baptism of the holy spirit of the Light, and there is a spiritual chrism; these lead the souls into the Treasury of the Light.' Tell us, therefore, their mystery, so that we ourselves may inherit the kingdom of thy father.*"

Jesus said unto them: "There is no mystery which is more excellent than these mysteries on which ye question, in that it will lead your souls into the Light of the lights, into the regions of Truth and Goodness, into the region of the Holy of all holies, into the region in which there is neither female nor male, nor are there forms in that region, but a perpetual indescribable Light. Nothing more excellent is there, therefore, than these mysteries on which ye question, save only the mystery of the seven Voices and their nine-and-forty powers and their ciphers. And there is no name which is more excellent than them all, the name in which are all names and all lights and all powers.

"Who then knoweth that name, if he cometh out of the body of matter, nor smoke nor darkness nor authority nor ruler of the Fate-sphere nor angel nor archangel nor power can hold down the soul which knoweth that name; but if it cometh out of the world and sayeth that name to the fire, it is quenched and the darkness withdraweth.

"And if it sayeth it to the demons and to the receivers of the outer darkness and their rulers and their authorities and their powers, they will all sink down and their flame will burn and they will cry out: 'Holy, holy art thou, most holy of all holies.'

"And if one sayeth that name to the receivers of the wicked chastisements and their authorities and all their powers and also to Barbelo and the invisible god and the three triple-powered gods, straightway if one will say this name in those regions, they will all fall one on another, will be undone and destroyed and cry out: 'O Light of all lights, which is in the boundless lights, remember us and purify us.'"

And when Jesus had finished saying these words, all his disciples wept with loud sobbing.

We see by reading further from the same text that Jesus did in fact possess a brilliant body of Light and that this Light body—and His very being—were in some mysterious manner bound up with the sun:

> *And that light-power came down over Jesus and surrounded him entirely, while he was seated removed from his disciples, and he had shone most exceedingly, and there was no measure for the light which was on him.*
>
> *And the disciples had not seen Jesus because of the great light in which he was, or which was about him; for their eyes were darkened because of the great light in which he was. But they saw only the light, which shot forth many light-rays. And the light-rays were not like one another, but the light was of divers kind, and it was of divers type, from below upwards, one more excellent than the other. . . in one great immeasurable glory of light; it stretched from under the earth right up to heaven. — And when the disciples saw that light, they fell into great fear and great agitation.*
>
> *It came to pass then, when that light-power had come down over Jesus, that it gradually surrounded him entirely. Then Jesus ascended or soared into the height, shining most exceedingly in an immeasurable light. And the disciples gazed after him and none of them spake, until he had reached unto heaven; but they all kept in deep silence. This then came to pass on the fifteenth day of the moon, on the day on which it is full in the month Tybi.*
>
> *It came to pass then, when Jesus had reached the heaven, after three hours, that all the powers of the heaven fell into agitation, and all were set in motion one against the other, they and all their aeons and all their regions and all their orders, and the whole earth was agitated and all they who dwell thereon. And all men who are in the world fell into agitation, and also the disciples, and*

all thought: Peradventure the world will be rolled up.

And all the powers in the heavens ceased not from their agitation, they and the whole world, and all were moved one against the other, from the third hour of the fifteenth day of the moon of Tybi until the ninth hour of the morrow. And all the angels and their archangels and all the powers of the height, all sang praises to the interiors of the interiors, so that the whole world heard their voices, without their ceasing till the ninth hour of the morrow.

But the disciples sat together in fear and were in exceedingly great agitation and were afraid because of the great earthquake which took place, and they wept together, saying: "What will then be? Peradventure the Saviour will destroy all regions?" Thus saying, they wept together.

While they then said this and wept together, then, on the ninth hour of the morrow, the heavens opened, and they saw Jesus descend, shining most exceedingly, and there was no measure for his light in which he was. For he shone more than at the hour when he had ascended to the heavens, so that men in the world cannot describe the light which was on him; and it shot forth light-rays in great abundance, and there was no measure for its rays, and its light was not alike together, but it was of divers kind and of divers type, some being more excellent than others. . . .

"Lo, I have then put on my Vesture, and all authority hath been given me through the First Mystery. Yet a little while and I will tell you the mystery of the universe and the stillness of the universe; and I will hide nothing from you from this hour on, but in fulness will I perfect you in all fulness and in all perfection and in all mysteries, which are the perfection of all perfections and the fulness of all fulnesses and the gnosis of all gnoses, — those which are in my Vesture. I will tell you all mysteries from

the exteriors of the exteriors to the interiors of the interiors. But hearken that I may tell you all things which have befallen me.

"*It came to pass then, when the sun had risen in the east, that a great light-power came down, in which was my Vesture, which I had left behind in the four-and-twentieth mystery, as I have said unto you.*"

7: MAN'S IMMORTAL NATURE

From the very earliest of times, chroniclers of Holy Scripture used the terms *fire* and *water* symbolically. The version of the story of Adam and Eve as found in the Book of Genesis of the Old Testament was only one of many versions recorded in ancient Scripture by writers of many civilizations. Undoubtedly, it is one of the oldest stories in the ancient world handed down by word of mouth from one generation to another, and it sheds some light on why these opposing elements were used. The *Two Books of Adam and Eve,* written in Arabic by an unknown Egyptian copyist (and later translated into other languages) give a more detailed and spiritually involved story than that recorded in Genesis. Parts of this account are found in the Qur-an (or Koran), the Talmud, and other ancient literature that deals with the story of how human life began in the universe. We have selected some passages that will help the reader to better understand the language within the language used by holy ones of times past.

The following lines from chapters 8 and 9 of the First Book tell of how the "Bright Nature" of humankind was taken away when Adam and Eve were cast out of the Garden, and of the water from the Tree of Life that gave birth to four rivers on earth. We are told that the original waters from the Tree of Life were a kind of light transformed into earthly water. That is why the prophets believed the water on earth was "moist light" and was used to purify unclean articles of clothing. Later, John the Baptist used water to wash away people's sins. This understanding stems from an ancient story in which it was believed that the earth was a copy of the original Garden of Eden but made of grosser material.

> *Then Adam wept and said, "O God, when we dwelt in the garden, and our hearts were lifted up, we saw the angels that sang praises in heaven, but now we do not see as we were used to do; nay, when we entered the cave, all creation became hidden from us.*
>
> *Then God the Lord said unto Adam, "When thou wast under subjection to Me, thou hadst a bright nature within thee, and for that reason couldst thou see things afar off. But after the transgression thy bright nature was withdrawn from thee; and it was not left to thee to see things afar off but only near at hand; after the ability of the flesh; for it is brutish.*
>
> *When Adam and Eve had heard these words from God, they went their way, praising and worshipping Him with a sorrowful heart.*
>
> *And God ceased to commune with them.*
>
> *Then Adam and Eve came out of the Cave of Treasures, and drew near to the garden gate, and there they stood to look at it, and wept for having come away from it.*
>
> *And Adam and Eve went from before the gate of the garden to the southern side of it, and found there the water that watered the garden, from the root of the Tree of Life, and that parted itself from thence into four rivers over the earth.*
>
> *Then Adam and Eve felt themselves burning with thirst, and heat, and sorrow.*

And Adam said to Eve, "We shall not drink of this water, even if we were to die, O Eve, when this water comes into our inner parts, it will increase our punishments and that of our children that shall come after us."

Both Adam and Eve then withdrew from the water, and drank none of it at all; but came and entered the Cave of Treasures.

But when in it Adam could not see; he only heard the noise she made. Neither could she see Adam, but heard the noise he made.

Then Adam wept, in deep affliction, and smote upon his breast; and he rose and said to Eve, "Where art thou?"

And she said unto him, "Lo, I am standing in this darkness."

He then said to her, "Remember the bright nature in which we lived, while we abode in the garden!

"O Eve! remember the glory that rested on us in the garden. O Eve! remember the trees that overshadowed us in the garden while we moved among them.

"O Eve! remember that while we were in the garden, we knew neither night nor day. Think of the Tree of Life, from below which flowed the water, and that shed lustre over us! Remember, O Eve, the garden land, and the brightness thereof!

"Think, oh think of that garden in which was no darkness, while we dwelt therein.

"Whereas no sooner did we come into this Cave of Treasures than darkness compassed us round about; until we can no longer see each other; and all the pleasure of this life has come to an end."

Then when God, who is merciful and full of pity, heard Adam's voice, He said unto him:

"O Adam, so long as the good angel was obedient to Me, a bright light rested on him and on his hosts.

"But when he transgressed My commandment, I deprived him of that bright nature, and he became dark.

"And when he was in the heavens, in the realms of light, he knew naught of darkness.

"But he transgressed, and I made him fall from heaven upon the earth; and it was this darkness that came upon him.

"And on thee, O Adam, while in My garden and obedient to Me, did that bright light rest also.

"But when I heard of thy transgression, I deprived thee of that bright light. Yet, of My mercy, I did not turn thee into darkness, but I made thee thy body of flesh, over which I spread this skin, in order that it may bear cold and heat.

"If I had let My wrath fall heavily upon thee, I should have destroyed thee; and had I turned thee into darkness, it would have been as if I killed thee.

"But in My mercy, I have made thee as thou art; when thou didst transgress My commandment, O Adam, I drove thee from the garden, and made thee come forth into this land; and commanded thee to dwell in this cave; and darkness came upon thee, as it did upon him who transgressed My commandment.

"Thus, O Adam, has this night deceived thee. It is not to last forever; but is only of twelve hours: when it is over, daylight will return.

Sigh not, therefore, neither he moved; and say not in the heart that this darkness is long and drags on wearily; and say not in thy heart that I plague thee with it.

"Strengthen thy heart, and be not afraid. This darkness is not a punishment. But, O Adam, I have made the day, and have placed the sun in it to give light; in order that thou and thy children should do your work.

"For I knew thou shouldest sin and transgress, and come out into this land. Yet would I not force thee, nor be heard upon thee, nor shut up; nor doom thee through thy fall; nor through thy coming out from light into darkness; nor yet through thy coming from the garden into this land.

"For I made thee of the light; and I willed to bring out children of light from thee and like unto thee.

"But thou didst not keep one day My commandment; until I had finished the creation and blessed everything in it.

"Then I commanded thee concerning the tree, that thou eat not thereof. Yet I knew that Satan, who deceived himself would also deceive thee.

"So I made known to thee by means of the tree, not to come near him. And I told thee not to eat of the fruit thereof nor to taste of it, nor yet to sit under it, nor to yield to it.

"Had I not been and spoken to thee, O Adam, concerning the tree, and had I left thee without a commandment, and thou hadst sinned—it would have been an offence on My part, for not having given thee any order; thou wouldst turn round and blame Me for it.

"But I commanded thee, and warned thee, and thou didst fall. So that My creatures cannot blame me; but the blame rests on them alone.

> "And, O Adam, I have made the day for thee and for thy children after thee, for them to work, and toil therein. And I have made the night for them to rest in it from their work; and for the beasts of the field to go forth by night and seek their food.
>
> "But little of darkness now remains, O Adam; and daylight will soon appear."

God then promises to send forth His own nature, the Word, into the world, to be manifest in the seed of Adam. Here we have a very early mention of a divine being to be sent to humankind. The following lines are taken from chapter 14:

> Then Adam said unto God: "O Lord, take Thou my soul and let me not see this gloom any more; or remove me to some place where there is no darkness.
>
> But God the Lord said to Adam, "Verily I say unto thee, this darkness pass from thee, every day I have determined for thee, until the fulfilment of My covenant; when I will save thee and bring thee back again into the garden, into the abode of light thou longest for, wherein is no darkness. I will bring thee to it—in the kingdom of heaven."
>
> Again said God unto Adam, "All this misery that thou hast been made to take upon thee because of thy transgression, will not free thee from the hand of Satan, and will not save thee."
>
> "But I will. When I shall come down from heaven, and shall become flesh of thy seed, and take upon Me the infirmity from which thou sufferest, then the darkness that came upon thee in this cave shall come upon Me in the grave, when I am in the flesh of thy seed.
>
> "And I, who am without years, shall be subject to the reckoning of years, of times, of months, and of days, and I shall be reckoned as one of the sons of men, in order to save thee."

And God ceased to commune with Adam.

We next learn of the first mention of the material sun—when Adam first saw it. It is representative of primordial fire and heat; another form of God's Light that existed in the Garden. These lines are taken from chapter 16:

After this Adam and Eve ceased not to stand in the cave, praying and weeping, until the morning dawned upon them.

And when they saw the light returned to them, they restrained from fear, and strengthened their hearts.

Then Adam began to come out of the cave. And when he came to the mouth of it, and stood and turned his face towards the east, and saw the sun rise in glowing rays, and felt the heat thereof on his body, he was afraid of it, and thought in his heart that this flame came forth to plague him.

He wept then, and smote upon his breast, and fell upon the earth on his face, and made his request saying:

"O Lord, plague me not, neither consume me, nor yet take away my life from the earth."

For he thought the sun was God.

Inasmuch as while he was in the garden and heard the voice of God and the sound He made in the garden, and feared Him, Adam never saw the brilliant light of the sun, neither d the flaming heat thereof touch his body.

Therefore was he afraid of the sun when flaming rays of it reached him. He thought God meant to plague him therewith all the days He had decreed for him.

For Adam also said in his thoughts, as God did not plague us with darkness, behold, He has caused this sun to rise and to plague us with burning heat.

> But while he was thus thinking in his heart, the Word of God came unto him and said:
>
> "O Adam, arise and stand up. This sun is not God; but it has been created to give light by day, of which I spake unto thee in the care saying, 'that the dawn would break forth, and there would be light by day.'
>
> "But I am God who comforted thee in the night."
>
> And God ceased to commune with Adam.

Lines from chapter 4 describe the painful realization of Adam and Eve that their "Bright Nature" has left them, and that they are now physical beings:

> And Adam said to Eve, "Look at thine eyes, and at mine, which afore beheld angels in heaven, praising; and they, too, without ceasing.
>
> "But now we do not see as we did: our eyes have become of flesh; they cannot see in like manner as they saw before.
>
> Adam said again to Eve, "What is our body today, compared to what it was in former days, when we dwelt in the garden?"

In chapter 64 we learn of Adam and Eve's attempts to eat their first earthly food, and of how the taste of bread and blood was added. Up to this time they had lived off the Light, and the light of the sun, indicated by their ritual of facing the sun at sunrise and sunset and offering prayers to God:

> Then God looked upon Adam and upon his strength of mind, upon his endurance of hunger and thirst, and of the heat. And he changed the two fig-trees into two figs, as they were at first, and then said to Adam and to Eve, "Each of you may take one fig." And they took them, as the Lord commanded them.

And he said to them, "Go ye into the cave, and eat the figs, and satisfy your hunger, lest ye die."

So, as God commanded them, they went into the cave, about the time when the sun was setting. And Adam and Eve stood up and prayed at the time of the setting sun.

Then they sat down to eat the figs; but they knew not how to eat them; for they were not accustomed to eat earthly food. They feared also lest, if they ate, their stomach should be burdened and their flesh thickened, and their hearts take to liking earthly food.

But while they were thus seated, God, out of pity for them, sent them His angel, lest they should perish of hunger and thirst.

And the angel said unto Adam and Eve, "God says to you that ye have not strength to fast until death; eat, therefore, and strengthen your bodies; for ye are now animal flesh that cannot subsist without food and drink."

Then Adam and Eve took the figs and began to eat of them. But God had put into them a mixture as of savoury bread and blood.

Chapter 65 adds to the story of eating the first food and the after-effects:

And when it was day, they rose and prayed, after their custom, and then went out of the cave.

But as they felt great trouble from the food they had eaten, and to which they were not used, they went about in the cave saying to each other:

"What has happened to us through eating, that this pain should have come upon us? Woe be to us, we shall die! Better for us to have died than to have eaten; and to have kept our bodies pure, than to have defiled them with food."

> *Then they prayed to God that He would have mercy on them; after which, their mind was quieted, their hearts were broken, and their longing was cooled down; and they were like strangers on earth. That night Adam and Eve spent in the cave, where they slept heavily by reason of the food they had eaten.*

And Adam and Eve drink water for the first time, as related in chapter 66:

> *When it was morning, the day after they had eaten food, Adam and Eve prayed in the cave, and Adam said unto Eve, "Lo, we asked for food of God, and He gave it. But now let us also ask Him to give us a drink of water."*

> *Then they arose, and went to the bank of the stream of water, that was on the south border of the garden, in which they had before thrown themselves. And they stood on the bank, and prayed to God that He would command them to drink of the water.*

> *Then the Word of God came to Adam, and said unto him, "O Adam, thy body is become brutish, and requires water to drink. Take ye, and drink, thou and Eve; give thanks and praise."*

> *Adam and Eve then drew near, and drank of it, until their bodies felt refreshed. After having drunk, they praised God, and then returned to their cave, after their former custom.*

The above quotations indicate the spiritual origins of humans and their degeneration from beings of Light to a grosser nature of flesh and bones. Since the time of the fall of Adam, ancient humans have been obsessed with atonement for the great sin of disobedience that has come to be known as original sin. The singular sin-offering was the blood of a sacrificed animal, done according to proper ritual and ceremony by authorized priests in a temple consecrated to God.

Christianity taught that Jesus was the Word of God come to Earth in human form; thus He had a spiritual as well as a human nature. The two indwelling natures—the spiritual and human—later became a theological matter that was debated for centuries, and still is. If Jesus was God incarnate in the flesh, then His spiritual nature did not die, or even suffer on the cross. It was the human nature that suffered and died. Thus, the blood shed during His crucifixion was to be a final atonement. Sacrifice no longer need be practiced. The form that appeared following the crucifixion was the spiritual Light body that was the true and original nature given to man in the Garden of Eden. That Jesus rose from the dead in spiritual form was indication that God had restored the original nature of humankind through the New Way that Jesus announced and taught. This New Way was a restoration of the Tree of Life, of which all people could eat and become immortal.

The eating of the flesh and the drinking of the blood, as emphasized by the evangelists, were allegorical terms used to show that a divine being had come in the flesh so that the shedding of the incarnate Word was the final and ultimate sacrifice. Humans were washed clean of sin forever by the supreme sacrifice. There was no other way for Jesus to teach His disciples; nor for the disciples to teach the greater masses of devout Jews (and later Gentiles) that blood sacrifice was no longer necessary or acceptable to God.

The sacrifice of the material body of Jesus was unimportant, except to replace animal sacrifice forever. It was the New Way that was important: that it was the grace of God that fulfilled the old Law and instructed the human family how to share in that grace. The psychology of the human mind is such that it becomes accustomed to traditional teachings, which are not easily replaced by new ones. For this reason, the life of Jesus was dramatic and dynamic, and in many ways bound up with the lives and teachings of many ancient teachers and gods who had become mythical as well as authoritative. Jesus filled the same roles as Mithra, Attis, Osiris, among other ancient figures who lived in times past. The stories of some of these figures were known and recorded among the Mediterranean peoples in the time of Jesus, but there were other stories and records from places like India, China, Mexico, and Peru that were unknown to them. In almost all cases, the teachings of the figures in these lands were in many ways similar to those of Jesus, which shows the continuity of the long line of saviors who came into the world and appear to have reached a culmination with the life of Jesus. Like the story of Adam and Eve in the Garden, the story of Jesus is representative of an ancient story that goes far back into time and is recorded by many peoples. The story is always the same.

Jesus came to teach that the Light of God that nourishes and sustains humankind's spiritual nature—their true and original nature given them in the beginning—was extended again by God and shed upon the world. But since humans have two natures, the Light and the Dark, in addition to the human nature, they are subject to certain laws governing the partaking of that divine Light and nourishment.

What was the nature of this divine Light? How was humanity to partake of it? From a reading of scripture, it is apparent that Jesus and His immediate disciples knew the secret. Ordinary humans were changed by that Light into supranormal humans. Sinners became prophets. Moreover, they became people of God, sharing in the divine nature and immortality. Such a nature did not come from obeying the Law nor by believing that Jesus was God incarnate nor by the performance of a symbolic ritual of sacrifice—there was more to it than that.

The wooden cross and the sacrifice of Jesus the man were substituted for the cross of Light that symbolized God's gift of grace, because primitive minds were obsessed by the symbolic shedding of the blood with the tree-cross that bore Jesus. The partaking of the bread and wine that represented the body and blood of Jesus was a parallel to the partaking of the first food and drink by Adam and Eve.

In the beginning, this ritual was meant to take the place of the sin-offering of unleavened bread and animal sacrifice. In acting out the ritual, they gradually forgot the higher food—that divine nourishment shed upon the world, which was the Light of God. Thus began the degeneration, the great apostasy predicted by Jesus and His disciples, of the Christian Community known as Christ's Church.

Had Christians continued the New Way taught by Jesus, imitating the life He exemplified, a new world would have come into being as prophesied by Him. Jesus had not erred in promising the advent of God's Kingdom on earth. Rather, humankind failed to share in the benefits, and the world He promised failed to materialize. The secret teachings were distorted and perverted by false teachers inspired by the Powers of Darkness, who continually seek to keep humankind away from their "Bright Nature."

The gift of the Holy Spirit at Pentecost replaced forever the value of blood sacrifice. This gift was the Bread of Life come from the spiritual Light of God through the sun of the material world and was the true baptism of fire given for the purification of humankind to wash away their material, and Dark nature.

Over and over again we see how Christians and ancient humans all over the world paid reverence to the light of the sun. We have read how the Essenes, Therapeutae, and the residents of Qumran on the Dead Sea, the Gnostic adherents in Egypt, the Greeks, and Iranians, to name but a few, identified the Light with the sun. None worshiped the sun, for this was forbidden from earliest times as a form of idolatry and corruption. Moses warned the Hebrews not to worship any graven image: *lest thou lift thine eyes unto heaven, and when thou seest the sun, and the moon, and the* stars, even all the host of heaven shouldest be driven to worship them, and serve them, which the Lord thy God hath divided unto all nations under the whole heaven (Deuteronomy 4:19).

Ezekiel wrote to the house of Israel concerning a vision he had of the profanations of the Temple (Ezekiel 8:6–18):

> *He said furthermore unto me, Son of man, seest thou what they do? even the great abominations that the house of Israel committeth here, that I should go far off from my sanctuary but turn thee yet again, and thou shalt see greater abominations.*
>
> *And he brought me to the door of the court; and when I looked, behold a hole in the wall.*
>
> *Then said he unto me, Son of man, dig now in the wall: and when I had digged in the wall, behold a door,*
>
> *And he said unto me, Go in, and behold the wicked abominations that they do here,*
>
> *So I went in and saw; and behold every form of creeping things, and abominable beasts, and all the idols of the house of Israel, portrayed upon the wall round about.*
>
> *And there stood before them seventy men of the ancients of the house of Israel, and in the midst of them stood Jaazanrah the son of Shaphan, with every man his censer in his hand; and a thick cloud of incense went up.*
>
> *Then said he unto me, Son of man, hast thou seen what the ancients of the house of Israel do in the dark, every man in the chambers of his imagery? for they say, The LORD seeth us not; the LORD hath forsaken the earth.*
>
> *He said also unto me, Turn thee yet again, and thou shalt see greater abominations that they do.*

Then he brought me to the door of the gate of the Lord's house which was toward the north; and, behold, there sat women weeping for Tammuz.

Then said he unto me, Hast thou seen this, O son of man? turn thee yet again, and thou shalt see greater abominations than these,

And he brought me into the inner court of the LORD'S house, and, behold, at the door of the temple of the LORD, between the porch and the altar, were about five and twenty men, with their backs toward the temple of the LORD, and their faces toward the east; and they worshipped the sun toward the east.

Then he said unto me, Hast thou seen this, O son of man? Is it a light thing to the house of Judah that they commit the abominations which they commit here? for they have filled the land with violence, and have returned to provoke me to anger: and, lo, they put the branch to their nose,

Therefore will I also deal in fury: mine eye shall not spare, neither will I have pity: and though they cry in mine ears with a loud voice, yet will I not hear them.

Ezekiel emphasized that God had created the sun, and it was His Light that lighted humans, not the light of the sun by day nor the lesser light of the moon by night. The Angel of the Lord was no less appalled when the Jews worshiped King Herod as a god, instead of giving the glory to God (see Acts 12:22). No form of idolatry was permitted to the Jews.

It was not the light of the sun that was forbidden but the manner in which it was observed. Luke has Jesus tell us: *The light of the body is the eye: therefore when thine eye is single, thy whole body also is full of light; but when thine eye is evil, thy body also is full of* darkness. Take heed therefore that the light which is in thee be not darkness. If thy whole body therefore be full of light, having no part dark, the whole shall be full of light (Luke 11:34–36).

Wisdom is good with an inheritance: and by it there is profit to them that see the sun. . . . Truly the light is sweet, and a pleasant thing it is for the eyes to behold the sun. So reads the Old Testament wisdom of Ecclesiastes (Ecclesiastes 7:11; 11:7).

The 19th Psalm describes the tabernacle of the sun and of the Bridal-chamber with which we are already familiar:

> The heavens declare the glory of God; and the firmament sheweth his handywork.
>
> Day unto day uttereth speech, and night unto night sheweth knowledge.
>
> There is no speech nor language, where their voice is not heard.
>
> Their line is gone out through all the earth, and their words to the end of the world. In them hath he set a tabernacle for the sun,
>
> Which is as a bridegroom coming out of his chamber, and rejoiceth as a strong man to run a race.
>
> His going forth is from the end of the heaven, and his circuit unto the ends of it: and there is nothing hid from the heat thereof.
>
> The law of the LORD is perfect, converting the soul: the testimony of the LORD is sure, making wise the simple.
>
> The statutes of the LORD are right, rejoicing the heart: the commandment of the LORD is pure, enlightening the eyes.

The Pistis Sophia, which has been quoted in previous pages, has Jesus speaking about the high priest and king Melchizedek:

> *Hearken then, Mary, and give ear, all ye disciples: Before I made proclamation to all the rulers of the aeons and to all the rulers of the Fate and of the sphere, they were all bound in their bonds and in their spheres and in their seals, as Yew, the Overseer of the Light, had bound them from the beginning; and every one of them remained in his order, and every one journeyed according to his course, as Yew, the Overseer of the Light, had established them. And when the time of the number of Melchisedec, the great Receiver of the Light, came, he was wont to come into the midst of the aeons and of all the rulers who are bound in the sphere and in the Fate, and he carried away the purification of the light from all the rulers of the aeons and from all the rulers of the Fate and from those of the sphere—for he carried away then that which brings them into agitation—and he set in motion the hastener who is over them, and made them turn their circles swiftly, and he carried away their power which was in them and the breath of their mouth and the tears of their eyes and the sweat of their bodies.*
>
> *And Melchisedec, the Receiver of the Light, purifieth those powers and carrieth their light into the Treasury of the Light, while the servitors of all the rulers gather together all matter from them all.*

Melchizedek (or *Melchisedec*) is presented in the Pistis Sophia as the receiver of the Light. Genesis 14:18 presents him as the priest-king offering bread and wine, memorials of sacrifice, to the most high God:

> *And Melchizedek king of Salem brought forth bread and wine: and he was the priest of the most high God.*
>
> *And he blessed him* [Abram/Abraham], *and said, Blessed be Abram of the most high God, possessor of heaven and earth.*

The New Testament author of the Epistle to the Hebrews has Jesus assuming the title of high priest, after the order of Melchizedek, explaining the successorship thusly: '

> Seeing then that we have a great high priest, that is passed into the heavens, Jesus the Son of God, let us hold fast our profession.
>
> For we have not an high priest which cannot be touched with the feeling of our infirmities; but was in all points tempted like as we are, yet without sin.
>
> Let us therefore come boldly unto the throne of grace, that we may obtain mercy, and find grace to help in time of need.
>
> For every high priest taken from among men is ordained for men in things pertaining to God, that he may offer both gifts and sacrifices for sins:
>
> Who can have compassion on the ignorant, and on them that are out of the way; for that he himself also is compassed with infirmity.
>
> And by reason hereof he ought, as for the people, so also for himself, to offer for sins.
>
> And no man taketh this honour unto himself, but he that is called of God, as was Aaron.
>
> So also Christ glorified not himself to be made an high priest; but he that said unto him, Thou art my Son, to day have I begotten thee,
>
> As he saith also in another place, Thou art a priest forever after the order of Melchizedek. (Hebrews 4:14–5:6)

Continuing in chapter 6 of the same epistle, the author quickly points out that though Jesus succeeds the high priest in the traditional role,

He nevertheless represents something new. Here again we encounter the mystery of the divine Bread in allegorical terms:

> *Therefore leaving the principles of the doctrine of Christ, let us go on unto perfection; not laying again the foundation of repentance from dead works, and of faith toward God,*
>
> *Of the doctrine of baptisms, and of laying on of hands, and of resurrection of the dead, and of eternal judgment.*
>
> *And this will we do, if God permit.*
>
> *For it is impossible for those who were once enlightened, and have tasted of the heavenly gift, and were made partakers of the Holy Ghost,*
>
> *And have tasted the good word of God, and the powers of the world to come,*
>
> *If they shall fall away, to renew them again unto repentance; seeing they crucify to themselves the Son of God afresh, and put him to an open shame.* (Hebrews 6:1-6)

In other words, as the author explains in chapter 7:11- 28, Christians must free themselves from continued repentance and sacrifice and participate in the divine gift. Repentance and sacrifice are not a perfect offering to God; if they had been, there would have been no need of the ministry and sacrifice of Jesus:

> *If therefore perfection were by the Levitical priesthood, (for under it the people received the law,) what further need was there that another priest should rise after the order of Melchisedec, and not be called after the order of Aaron?*
>
> *For the priesthood being changed, there is made of necessity a change also of the law,*

For he of whom these things are spoken pertaineth to another tribe, of which no man gave attendance at the altar.

For it is evident that our Lord sprang out of Juda; of which tribe Moses spake nothing concerning priesthood.

And it is yet far more evident: for that after the similitude of Melchisedec there ariseth another priest,

Who is made, not after the law of a carnal commandment, but after the power of an endless life.

For he testifieth, Thou art a priest forever after the order of Melchisedec.

For there is verily a disannulling of the commandment going before for the weakness and unprofitableness thereof.

For the law made nothing perfect, but the bringing in of a better hope did; by the which we draw nigh unto God.

And inasmuch as not without an oath he was made priest:

(For those priests were made without an oath; but this with an oath by him that said unto him, The Lord sware and will not repent, Thou art a priest forever after the order of Melchisedec:)

By so much was Jesus made a surety of a better testament,

And they truly were many priests, because they were not suffered to continue by reason of death:

But this man, because he continueth ever, hath an unchangeable priesthood.

Wherefore he is able also to save them to the uttermost that come unto God by him, seeing he ever liveth to make intercession for them,

For such an high priest became us, who is holy, harmless, undefiled, separate from sinners, and made higher than the heavens;

Who needeth not daily, as those high priests, to offer up sacrifice, first for his own sins, and then for the people's: for this he did once, when he offered up himself.

For the law maketh men high priests which have infirmity; but the word of the oath, which was since the law, maketh the Son, who is consecrated forevermore.

Chapter 8 (verses 1–28) of Hebrews emphasizes that the old Law was fulfilled with the advent of Jesus, who established a new covenant, thereby amending and supplementing the Law:

Now of the things which we have spoken this is the sum: We have such an high priest, who is set on the right hand of the throne of the Majesty in the heavens;

A minister of the sanctuary, and of the true tabernacle, which the Lord pitched, and not man.

For every high priest is ordained to offer gifts and sacrifices: wherefore it is of necessity that this man have somewhat also to offer.

For if he were on earth, he should not be a priest, seeing that there are priests that offer gifts according to the law:

Who serve unto the example and shadow of heavenly things, as Moses was admonished of God when he was about to make the tabernacle: for, See, saith he, that thou make all things according to the pattern shewed to thee in the mount.

But now hath he obtained a more excellent ministry, by how much also he is the mediator of a better covenant, which was established upon better promises.

For if that first covenant had been faultless, then should no place have been sought for the second,

For finding fault with them, he saith, Behold, the days come, with the Lord, when I will make a new covenant with the house of Israel and with the house of Judah:

Not according to the covenant that I made with their fathers in the day when I took them by the hand to lead them out of the land of Egypt; because they continued not in my covenant, and I regarded them not, saith the Lord.

For this is the covenant that I will make with the house of Israel after those days, saith the Lord; I will put my laws into their mind, and write them in their hearts: and I will be to them a God, and they shall be to me a people:

And they shall not teach every man his neighbour, and every man his brother, saying, Know the Lord: for all shall know me, from the least to the greatest.

For I will be merciful to their unrighteousness, and their sins and their iniquities will I remember no more.

In that he saith, A new covenant, he hath made the first old. Now that which decayeth and waxeth old is ready to vanish away.

The account continues in the ninth chapter (verses 11–28) where the author attempts to show the Jews that a type of final sin-offering has been made and that Jesus has instituted a new order. Finally, Christ is to come a second time for the salvation of the world. We thus learn that the Second Advent is a necessary step in the total fulfillment of God's plan for humanity:

But Christ being come an high priest of good things to come, by a greater and more perfect tabernacle, not made with hands, that is to say, not of this building;

Neither by the blood of goats and calves, but by his own blood he entered in once into the holy place, having obtained eternal redemption for us.

For if the blood of bulls and of goats, and the ashes of an heifer sprinkling the unclean, sanctifieth to the purifying of the flesh:

How much more shall the blood of Christ, who through the eternal Spirit offered himself without spot to God, purge your conscience from dead works to serve the living God?

And for this cause he is the mediator of the new testament, that by means of death, for the redemption of the transgressions that were under the first testament, they which are called might receive the promise of eternal inheritance.

For where a testament is, there must also of necessity be the death of the testator.

For a testament is of force after men are dead: otherwise it is of no strength at all while the testator liveth.

Whereupon neither the first testament was dedicated without blood,

For when Moses had spoken every precept to all the people according to the law, he took the blood of calves and of goats, with water, and scarlet wool, and hyssop, and sprinkled both the book, and all the people,

Saying, This is the blood of the testament which God hath enjoined unto you.

Moreover he sprinkled with blood both the tabernacle, and all the vessels of the ministry.

And almost all things are by the law purged with blood; and without shedding of blood is no remission.

> *It was therefore necessary that the patterns of things in the heavens should be purified with these; but the heavenly things themselves with better sacrifices than these,*
>
> *For Christ is not entered into the holy places made with hands, which are the figures of the true; but into heaven itself, now to appear in the presence of God for us:*
>
> *Nor yet that he should offer himself often, as the high priest entereth into the holy place every year with blood of others;*
>
> *For then must he often have suffered since the foundation of the world: but now once in the end of the world hath he appeared to put away Sin by the sacrifice of himself.*
>
> *And as it is appointed unto men once to die, but after this the judgment:*
>
> *So Christ was once offered to bear the sins of many; and unto them that look for him shall he appear the second time without sin unto salvation.*

These words make it exceedingly clear that the sacrifice of bread and wine, of flesh and blood, was of the old Law from which all Christians, both Jew and non-Jew were now free. Therefore, the ritual of the last supper, the Communion in which the bread and wine became the flesh and blood of Jesus through transubstantiation, which has come down to modern-day Christians, was probably no more than an allegorical or symbolic ceremony done in memory of Jesus to forever erase from the mind of the adherent the need for any kind of blood sacrifice, whether the adherent be a Jew, Mithrite, or member of any other of the old religions.

Jesus and His disciples, including Paul, offered a much higher communion to the followers of the New Way. No ritual or ceremony could accomplish this new birth in which the adherent walked in fellowship with God as a new spiritual being. It was more than likely that the catechumens received the preliminary catechism of Jesus before being admitted to communicant membership in the Christian Community. This catechesis consisted of basic doctrines, the milk for babes not yet ready for the meat of the teaching, which in all probability included an acting out or ritual in which the adherent partook of the bread and wine which became the flesh and blood of Jesus —the ultimate sin-offering through the act of transubstantiation, in order to put out of people's minds the need for actual blood sacrifice of lamb, bull, or other animal in the many religions of the time.

Paul makes clear the sharp division that existed between the initiates who had to be weaned from their pagan or Jewish beliefs and those who were enlightened by Christ. We quote from Paul's First Epistle to the Corinthians (1 Cor. 2:14–3:3):

> *But the natural man receiveth not the things of the Spirit of God: for they are foolishness unto him: neither can he know them, because they are spiritually discerned.*
>
> *But he that is spiritual judgeth all things, yet he himself is judged of no man,*
>
> *For who hath known the mind of the Lord, that he may instruct him? But we have the mind of Christ.*
>
> *And I, brethren, could not speak unto you as unto spiritual, but as unto carnal, even as unto babes in Christ.*
>
> *I have fed you with milk, and not with meat: for hitherto ye were not able to bear it, neither yet now are ye able.*
>
> *For ye are yet carnal: for whereas there is among you envying, and strife, and divisions, are ye not carnal, and walk as men?*

What was this "meat" that the initiates were not able to bear? We know from an earlier quotation from the same epistle (11:27–30) that the bread and wine of the new covenant was not a ritual, as commonly supposed, but something that the participant could only receive under certain conditions:

> *Wherefore whosoever shall eat this bread, and drink this cup of the Lord, unworthily, shall be guilty of the body and blood of the Lord.*
>
> *But let a man examine himself, and so let him eat of that bread, and drink of that cup.*
>
> *For he that eateth and drinketh unworthily, eateth and drinketh damnation to himself, not discerning the Lord's body.*
>
> *For this cause many are weak and sickly among you, and many sleep.*

Paul himself suffered a similar fate during his early ministry—probably on the road to Damascus. In his Epistle to the Galatians (4:13–15) he openly confesses the infirmity he bore:

> *Ye know how through infirmity of the flesh I preached the gospel unto you at the first.*
>
> *And my temptation which was in my flesh ye despised not, nor rejected; but received me as an angel of God, even as Christ Jesus.*
>
> *Where is then the blessedness ye spake of? for I bear you record, that, if it had been possible, ye would have plucked out your own eyes, and have given them to me.*

That Paul's eyes were affected is evidenced at the end of the letter (6:11) when he declares: *Ye see how large a letter I have written unto you with mine own hand.* Usually, Paul dictated his letters, but in the absence of a secretary he took up the pen and wrote with blurred vision. He made his point to the Galatians, for he ended the letter with the words: *From henceforth let no man trouble me:*

for I bear in my body the marks of the Lord Jesus. There is little doubt that he refers to his vision of Jesus appearing out of the sky in a dazzling light that shone more brilliant than the midday sun, resulting in his temporary blindness for having persecuted the disciples of the Lord. We can assume that something of the condition reappeared in his later years.

Paul, evidently troubled by persecution and knowing that his letters might fall into the hands of the authorities, did not use clear speech, electing instead to use the secret symbols with which he was familiar, shrouding his words in cryptic language so that only those familiar with the oral teachings could possibly understand their meaning. This was a familiar device used by all the evangelists. If our impression that Paul used allegory throughout his writings is correct (the following passages show that he was familiar with its use), then we can assume that the mention of the bread and the wine and their relation to the body and blood of Jesus was allegorical with a hidden meaning. Obviously, Paul attributed a dual nature to Jesus —the human and the divine. We read in Galatians 4:22–25:

> *For it is written, that Abraham had two sons, the one by a bondmaid, the other by a freewoman.*
>
> *But he who was of the bondwoman was born after the flesh; but he of the freewoman was by promise.*
>
> *Which things are an allegory: for these are the two covenants; the one from the mount Sinai, which gendereth to bondage, which is Agar.*
>
> *For this Agar is mount Sinai in Arabia, and answereth to Jerusalem which now is, and is in bondage with her children.*

The fact that Jesus was crucified and shed His blood on the cross was understood and taught to be the final blood sacrifice, forever doing away with the blood sacrifice of animals and releasing humankind from the yoke of bondage. Primitive humanity, bound to pagan religions and those higher religions of the old Law, could understand such a teaching. The teaching was brilliant, meaningful, and above all, understandable to minds burdened with the blood religions of the day.

This represented the most rudimentary teaching. Freedom from the old teachings was a prerequisite to participating in the higher, spiritual teachings. We are not told in plain language what this higher spiritual teaching was. But it had something to do with the mystery of the new Bread of Life offered by God through Christ.

This Bread of Life offered by God through Christ was compared to the manna given by God to the Hebrews: the small, white food that tasted like honey-wafers. The banquets of the Mithrites and other religions included communal bread shaped in the form of a god, which when eaten by the elect, allowed them to take on the nature of the divine being. This was something the Jews, Greeks, Romans, Egyptians, and other Mediterranean peoples could understand. Be this as it may, these communal meals did not result in sickness or death if the communicant was found unworthy. This was one of the differences that separated the Christian message from other religions of the time.

John writes in his Book of Revelation (2:17): *He that hath an ear, let him hear what the Spirit saith unto the churches; To him that overcometh will I give to eat of the hidden manna, and will give him a white stone, and in the stone a new name written, which no man knoweth saving he that receiveth it.* John's Gospel illustrates this message with the following exchange between Jesus and the Jews (John 6:31–33): *Our fathers did eat manna in the desert; as it is written, He gave them bread from heaven to eat. Then Jesus said unto them, Verily, verily, I say unto you, Moses gave you not that bread from heaven; but my Father giveth you the true bread from heaven. For the bread of God is he which cometh down from heaven, and giveth life unto the world.*

The feeding of the five thousand, and again of the four thousand, by Jesus, parallels the manna given to the Hebrews in the desert wilderness. We have here a symbolic act, as opposed to a historical fact, which involves the secret mystery of the Eucharist, which was the most fundamental rite of Christianity. The hidden manna, the divine food offered by God to the Children of Light, represents something entirely different from that represented in the neo-Christian communion of bread and wine. The allegorical language of the evangelical accounts describing the arcane parables of Jesus concealed a veiled truth that was the key to the spiritual growth of the first Christians. They were privileged to receive the oral teachings that threw light upon the otherwise unintelligible writings delivered by the Apostles for reading in the communities given over to the mystery. This veiled truth is evident throughout the New Testament to anyone who has the key to unlock the coded steganographic messages of the writings.

John's Christology expressed in his spiritual Gospel on *the living bread which came down from heaven: if any man eat of this bread, he shall live forever: . . .* gives us a clue to the nature of the secret Eucharist as taught by the Apostles. It was a divine nourishment that gave growth to the spiritual faculties and made people new creatures.

There was great interest in magical arts in those times, religions and philosophies were as numerous as the stars, and every teacher who offered a unique way to salvation or who dabbled in exorcism, magic, fortune-telling, astrology, or metaphysics, no matter how odd, was assured a following. Therefore, when the Apostles preached in the metropolises of the Greeks, Romans, Egyptians, Babylonians, Syrians, or any other of the great centers of Asia or Europe, they were confronted by sophisticated people who believed in some art or religion, and the Apostles were therefore viewed with suspicion.

But the Apostles were aided by the cosmic Christ and many signs were given in their favor. Those who opposed them, or those who attempted to pervert their teachings or use the name of Jesus in vain or for clandestine reasons, came to no good end. We have an account of this in Acts (19:13–19):

> *Then certain of the vagabond Jews, exorcists, took upon them to call over them which had evil spirits the name of the Lord Jesus, saying, We adjure you by Jesus whom Paul preacheth.*
>
> *And there were seven sons of one Sceva, a Jew, and chief of the priests, which did so.*
>
> *And the evil spirit answered and said, Jesus I know, and Paul I know; but who are ye?*
>
> *And the man in whom the evil spirit was leaped on them, and overcame them, and prevailed against them, so that they fled out of that house naked and wounded.*
>
> *And this was known to all the Jews and Greeks also dwelling at Ephesus; and fear fell on them all, and the name of the Lord Jesus was magnified.*
>
> *And many that believed came, and confessed, and shewed their deeds.*
>
> *Many of them also which used curious arts brought their books together, and burned them before all men: and they counted the price of them, and found it fifty thousand pieces of silver.*

The religion of Jesus, then, was a Light religion in which the Angels of Light and the Powers of Light bestowed divine credentials upon the disciples. Their preaching of the immortality of the human soul was revolutionary because their immortality was experienced by the believers while they lived on earth. Unlike the sorcerers or teachers of strange religions who promised immortality in the hereafter, Christianity was a living religion in the here and now. Early Christianity was a cosmic religion of the first magnitude because it had a following of believers who applied the system taught by Jesus. Here was a divine marriage in which heaven and earth were united. Had the religion spread, the Kingdom of God would have been reestablished on earth as promised by Jesus.

The performance of miracles was not an integral part of the teaching. The miracle was the New Life as taught by Christ and the restoration of humankind's divine nature through God. It became the goal of the Apostles and their followers to bring all people, Gentile and Jew, pagan and mystic, magician and sorcerer, those who had been under the Law as well as those who were ignorant of it, into the New Way for Christ's sake. Unfortunately, the Apostles were martyred and their closest disciples killed. In this way, the keys to the teachings were lost. What survived—that which was passed down to the greater masses or heirs to the Christian message as given by those in authoritative positions ignorant of the New Way—consisted of corrupted teachings that barely touched on the original basic teachings. The heart of the message perished. As a result, the promised Kingdom failed to materialize, not through any fault of Jesus or the Apostles, but by humanity's failure to preserve the teachings and apply them as instructed.

The later Christians who expected the appearance of Jesus and the Kingdom waited in vain (as they are still doing today). They were not aware that humankind itself is the recipient of God's salvation as announced by Christ, and it is only humans, individually and collectively, who can bring it about by applying certain cosmic principles made available nearly two thousand years ago through inspired men under Jesus. God did not restore Adam and Eve in the allegorical Garden of Eden following the Fall. God will not restore humankind today. The whole meaning of Christ's Appearance is to teach the existence of God's grace shed upon the earth, and the proper formula for involving humanity in this divine grace. Therefore, humankind's destiny is left entirely in its own hands within the greater Godhead, as it has been since the beginning of humanity's fall from grace.

8: CHRISTIANITY AND GOD'S SUN

Christ was associated with the sun throughout the ancient Christian writings. This is particularly true of, but not limited to, the disputed and unauthorized books known as the Apocrypha and Pseudepigrapha, those hidden and pseudonymous texts that are coming to the attention of scholars, and without which a proper understanding of early Christianity and the New Testament is not possible. The earliest mention of the Messianic Sun comes from the last book of the canonical Old Testament, the Prophet Malachi (4:1–6):

> *For, behold, the day cometh, that shall burn as an oven; and all the proud, yea, and all that do wickedly, shall be stubble: and the day that cometh shall burn them up, saith the LORD of hosts, that it shall leave them neither root nor branch.*
>
> *But unto you that fear my name shall the Sun of righteousness arise with healing in his wings; and ye shall go forth, and grow up as calves of the stall.*
>
> *And ye shall tread down the wicked; for they shall be ashes under the soles of your feet in the day that I shall do this, saith the LORD of hosts.*

> *Remember ye the law of Moses my servant, which I commanded unto him in Ho-reb for all Israel, with the statutes and judgments.*
>
> *Behold, I will send you Eliijah the prophet before the coming of the great and dreadful day of the LORD:*
>
> *And he shall turn the heart of the fathers to the children, and the heart of the children to their fathers, lest I come and smite the earth with a curse.*

These lines tell us that on the Great Day of the Lord, the Messianic Sun of Righteousness will shine forth, illuminating the whole universe with the Light of God. This is to be the final coming of Christ (God's mediating force given for the sake of humankind), not in the form of a man as before, but in the form of Light, in which God shall be incarnate in a great new spiritual Sun, unlike any sun that has ever shone before. Therefore, it will not be a new man-savior come into the world to redeem mankind, but God manifesting in nature and directly uplifting the spirits of humanity through a Spiritual Light. Needless to say, those who previously held the office of Christ, and all the prophets and holy ones redeemed by God, will be part of this great New Age, God's Christ Age, for the creation of a new community.

The monks of Qumran sang these lines from the Scroll of the War of the Sons of Light against the Sons of Darkness:

> *[He] shall shine upon all the ends of the world, shining ever more brightly till the times of darkness be over. And in God's appointed time His exalted majesty will illumine all the extremities of the world for peace and blessing, for honour and joy, and length of days for all the Sons of Light.*

The Book of the Secrets of Enoch refers to the New Sun:

And when the Lord shall send a great light, then there will be judgement for the just and the unjust, and there no one shall escape notice.

The Hymns of the Qumran Community also refer to it:

A source of light shall become an eternal ever-flowing fountain, and in its bright flames all the sons of iniquity shall be consumed. It shall be a fire to devour all sinful men in utter destruction.

Isaiah mentions the Messianic Sun (24:23) : *Then the moon shall be confounded, and the sun ashamed, when the Lord of Hosts shall reign.* Isaiah also predicts that *the light of the moon shall be as the light of the sun, and the light of the sun shall be sevenfold, as the light of seven days, in the day that the Lord bindeth up the breach of his people* (30:26), and the Talmud comments on these lines, saying they refer to the messianic years and the former to the world to come (Sanhedrin 91b). We have here a spiritual Sun in which God shall incarnate in sunlight and in the energy of every atom, shedding His grace upon every living thing. Those of the spirit, the Elect of God, shall see this Light. The parable of the sower spoken by Jesus to the multitude beside the sea in Matthew 13:3–6 reflects this teaching symbolically:

Behold, a sower went forth to sow; And when he sowed, some seeds fell by the way side, and the fowls came and devoured them up: Some fell upon stony places, where they had not much earth: and forthwith they sprang up, because they had no deepness of earth: And when the sun was up, they were scorched and because they had no root, they withered away.

As with physical sight, so with spiritual sight. If people with physical sight, unlike the blind, are forced to inhabit dark places, they will still have vision to see when the light is restored. The spiritually blind will not see the Light, though they will be changed by it and come to grief as a moth come to the flame. The spiritually blind will imitate the episode in the Garden of Eden and continue to eat of the Tree of Knowledge of Good and Evil instead of from the Tree of Life, which shall be bestowed upon the Righteous, who will become immortal as God intended them to be.

In the ancient philosophies and religions of the world, light was held to be the carrier of the divine Word, or Logos. The Phoenicians declared that the rays of Light are the purest incarnation of the divine intelligence. Though this Light was invisible and generated by God from spiritual realms, it nevertheless was interrelated or bound up with the visible light of the physical universe. The Romans called this higher sun the Sun of intellect. Thus our parent sun and stars, as sources of physical or visible light, were pumps or valves through which the invisible manifested. This is especially true of the sun, which is the greatest focal point of energy exchange in the solar system, and is therefore, the greatest source of visible light and invisible Light known to humankind. We see, then, there was a Sun within the sun, the visible being mixed with the invisible.

It was natural that ancient peoples looked to the light of the sun as cocreator of life on the planet. All living things on the face of the earth, and even under the sea, are dependent upon sunlight for existence. Though sunlight, without which nothing could survive, is relatively simple in appearance, it is nevertheless responsible for complex forms of living species. We see that sunlight, therefore, must be the carrier of some form or forms of intelligence. Sunlight is more than a source of stimuli that act upon living organisms; it has the capacity to cause an organism to respond in a certain way; e.g., photosynthesis in plants. Thus it was only natural for primitive people to look upward to the sun, for sunlight had evolved the eyes that fed the brain and the mind, via the nervous system, with e energy, making thoughts and actions possible. Humans, inwardly aware of the creative nature of the sun, knew they were linked to the mighty source of all light and heat upon the earth and worshiped the sun as the visible instrument of God. Indeed all sources of light—the nighttime moon, planets, and stars—were believed to be agents of God, each having its own distinctive effect on living things. Thus began humankind's communion with light as a means of knowing and understanding the invisible God.

When the sun was darkened for some inexplicable reason, as ancient writings and our own scientific information say it was, the earth was gripped in the cold of ice ages, and people grew fearful that the sun would go out forever, never to return. Believing that they had somehow sinned against this all-seeing eye of God, the people sacrificed to it, invoking it with gifts to return. When the sun emerged again, shedding its benevolent light upon its subjects, vegetation burst forth, and the earth was joyful. To commemorate the event, artificial hills were built, and temples facing the sun were constructed atop them in the hope of renewing humanity's communion with the Great Spirit of Light responsible for giving them visible light and heat.

Ancient prophets and philosophers taught that humans were made in the image of God, not as a physical being, for the physical body was related to the lesser nature of man, but as a Light body made in the image of the Greater Light of God and that was more akin to the Spiritual Consciousness that gave humans their immortal spirits. This Light body was the archetype of physical humanity—people's true nature—from which had devolved the physical form through some fault or sin against God. The Word of God, the Logos, the divine Light that shone brilliantly upon humans' spiritual nature, feeding their spirit and giving them conscious life. The ancient writings and myths all report that at one time the whole universe was illuminated by the invisible

Light of God, when humans, as Light beings, walked in fellowship with God. Adam Kadmon, the First archetypal Man, lived under this primordial Sun of God, the First invisible Light, which was the Tree of Life that shed its fruit for the nourishment of Adam. With his fall from God's grace, Adam was given a lesser light, the physical sun, and the First Light body took on visible form, which was dependent upon the visible sun as was the Light body upon the spiritual Light.

The visible sun was like a veil between Humanity and God, yet gave humankind life. The sun became the icon of God, the visible image, and in the absence of the Supreme Creator, which humans no longer knew, was held to be the divine mediator between humans and God. For this reason the light of the sun was sacred, and people reflected the light back to the source, believing that their bodies and their minds were descended from the sun, just as their spiritual consciousness and Light bodies had been fashioned from the Light of God, which they sought to reach through the mediating sun.

The early Christians believed that Christ, the Word (Logos or firstborn Son of God) that communes with the spirits of humans, came as the man Jesus. This spirit, come in flesh, sought to communicate a message to humankind. This message was to teach humanity how to feed upon the invisible Light that was being shed through the sun. Just as the spirit was present in the flesh, the invisible Light was present in the visible light of the sun. This theme is expressed in the words of the New Testament Epistle to the Philippians (2:5–11):

> *Let this mind be in you, which was also in Christ Jesus:*
>
> *Who, being in the form of God, thought it not robbery to be equal with God:*

> *But made himself of no reputation, and took upon him the form of a servant, and was made in the likeness of men:*
>
> *And being found in fashion as a man, he humbled himself, and became obedient unto death, even the death of the cross.*
>
> *Wherefore God also hath highly exalted him, and given him a name which is above every name:*
>
> *That at the name of Jesus every knee should bow, of things in heaven, and things in earth, and things under the earth;*
>
> *And that every tongue should confess that Jesus Christ is Lord, to the glory of God the Father.*

Neo-Christian theologians confused Jesus with God the Father because they did not have a full understanding of the cryptography used by the Gospel writers. What they failed to grasp was that the divine nature of the man Jesus was preexistent, come from the Worlds of Light and sent as a messenger to humankind. Angels who inhabit the Worlds of Light are the image (Word) of God, and therefore are identified with God yet are not God the Father. After the crucifixion of Jesus His divine nature was restored to the Light from which He had come. What was important was that the divine presence still remained in the sun, being accessible to all humankind equally. Therefore, the sun was the mediator, the bridge to God, wherein dwelled the spirit of Jesus and of all holders of the office of Christ who had come to humankind at the direction of God the Father. Light upon Light, the visible was mingled with the invisible; the physical and the divine being linked, as it had been with Jesus and the Godhead.

Thus we see that the Sun of Righteousness is the source of God's Light shed upon the whole world yet understood only by the Righteous or those knowledgeable in the sacred sciences; all others are blind to it. That is why the author of the Epistle to the

Ephesians urged his readers with this quote from a hymn: *Awake thou that sleepest, and arise from the dead, and Christ shall give thee Light* (5:14).

John, in symbolical style, explains how darkness fails to acknowledge Christ (John 1:1–5):

> *In the beginning was the Word, and the Word was with God, and the Word was God.*
>
> *The same was in the beginning with God.*
>
> *All things were made by him; and without him was not any thing made that was made.*
>
> *In him was life; and the life was the light of men.*
>
> *And the light shineth in darkness; and the darkness comprehended it not.*

From earliest times, Christ has been identified not only with our parent sun, but also with the promised Sun of Righteousness that was destined to rise in the east through the physical sun. With the appearance of the Sun of Righteousness, the earth will experience a kind of spiritual heat that will affects the souls of humankind. Eventually, the physical sun is destined to be affected by the source of all Light; the earth and all living things will be reduced to cinders, the oceans dissolved, and the earth dried up along with all physical life. Yet, humanity will not die, but be transformed. The earth shall become as the sun, being all light, and only the Light People will survive the holocaust. In those days the Power of Darkness will be conquered and humankind restored to its natural state of Light.

Isaiah records this promised event with the following words (60:19–21):

The sun shall be no more thy light by day; neither for brightness shall the moon give light unto thee: but the LORD shall be unto thee an everlasting light, and thy God thy glory.

Thy sun shall no more go down; neither shall thy moon withdraw itself for the Lord) shall be thine everlasting light, and the days of thy mourning shall be ended,

Thy people also shall be all righteous: they shall inherit the land for ever, the branch of my planting, the work of my hands, that I may be glorified.

The words in Matthew's Gospel make clear the Christian attitude toward this event (13:40–43):

As therefore the tares are gathered and burned in the fire; so shall it be in the end of this world.

The Son of man shall send forth his angels, and they shall gather out of his kingdom all things that offend, and them which do iniquity;

And shall cast them into a furnace of fire; there shall be wailing and gnashing of teeth.

Then shall the righteous shine forth as the sun in the kingdom of their Father. Who hath ears to hear, let him hear.

This promised event was ritually acted out in the Roman Church at Easter, when the risen Christ was celebrated in ceremonies that united fire, sun, and spirit es . The rites of resurrection began at midnight between Holy Saturday and Easter Sunday. It was at this time that the catechumens, the white-robed ones to be initiated, were admitted into the Church as full communicants through Baptism. The lights in the church were extinguished, leaving the whole assembly in darkness. The officiating bishop then struck a flint, causing a spark to ignite a box of tinder, and there was new light.

Blowing upon the tinder, the bishop chanted a prayer:

> *Oh God who by thy Son, the Cornerstone, hast bestowed upon the faithful the fire of thy brightness, sanctify this new fire produced from a stone for our use; and grant that, during this Paschal [Easter]Festival, we may be so inflamed with heavenly desires, that with pure minds we may come to the solemnity of perpetual glory . . .*

and blessing the new fire, the bishop continued:

> *that not only the sacrifice which is offered this night may shine by Thy mysterious light; but also into whatever place anything of this mystical sanctification shall be brought, there, by the power of Thy majesty, all the malicious artifices of the devil may be defeated.*

Lighting coals in a censer from the little flame, the bishop then moved to a triple candle, and having lit one of the wicks listened reverently as the deacon intoned:

> *Lumen Christi!* (The Light of Christ!)

and the choir responded:

> *Deo Gratias!* (Thanks be to God!)

This was repeated twice more, once after each of the two remaining wicks of the triple candle were lit. Then the bishop moved to the large Paschal Candle that would burn for forty days, from Easter to the Ascension, as the deacon chanted the ancient Exsultet:

> *Rejoice now all ye heavenly legions of angels! Celebrate with joy the divine mysteries, and for the King that cometh with victory*

let the trumpet proclaim salvation. Rejoice, O earth, illumined by this celestial radiancy: and may the whole world know itself to be delivered from darkness, brightened by the glory of the Eternal King.

Later in the ceremony, the bishop chanted:

Who makes this water fruitful for the regeneration of men by the arcane admixture of his divine Power, to the end that those who have been conceived in sanctity in the immaculate womb of this divine Font, may be born a new creature, and come forth a heavenly offspring: and that all who are distinguished either in sex or in body, or by age in time, may be born into one infancy by grace, their mother. . . .

We are reminded of the words of the Epistle to the Ephesians (5:8–9):

For ye were sometimes in darkness, but now are ye light in the Lord: walk as children of light:

(For the fruit of the Spirit is in all goodness and righteousness and truth;)

The Exsultet continued:

Here may the stains of all sins be washed out: here may human nature, created in thine image, and reformed to the honour of its Principle, be cleansed from the entire squalor of the old man: that every one who enters into this sacrament of regeneration may be reborn into the new childhood of true innocence. Through our Lord Jesus Christ Thy Son: Who shall come to judge the living and the dead and the world by fire. Amen.

The ceremony concluded close to dawn, and then the Eucharist was celebrated. The peal of the church bells greeted the first light of the rising sun while the Eucharistic host was mounted in the center of a golden monstrance, fashioned like a radiant sunburst, and displayed to the assembly, who then partook of communion.

We have here a tradition that was preserved in the Church for centuries; from earliest times, the original Christians in Palestine were reported to have gathered on a fixed day before it was light to chant an antiphonal hymn to Christ, commemorating the Resurrection. Like the Essenes and Therapeutae before them, they offered prayers at dawn toward the rising sun with hands upheld to heaven, singing hymns of praise:

> *Thou hast shone upon me in thy power at dawn*

thereby giving thanks for the Messiah who had come into the world as promised by the prophets of old. And as was the custom of the Essenes (who celebrated events on days fixed by a solar calendar, unlike the priesthood at Jerusalem who used a more recently instituted lunar calendar), the early Christians would have honored the first day of the Easter season (the first Sunday following the first full moon after the vernal equinox) by chanting a hymn of praise for this occasion:

> *At all recurring times I will sing His decree—At the beginning of the rule of light, during its course, and at its withdrawal to the home assigned it: at the beginning of the watches of darkness, when, its storehouse opened, it is set on high, during its course and when withdrawn before the light; when the luminaries shine forth from the lofty abode of holiness and at their withdrawal to the house of glory; at the coming of the seasons on days of new moon, which unite their circuits with their bonds, each with each; when they come round again there is a great day for the Holy of Holies.*

> *And a glorious sign of the release of His eternal mercies; at the beginning of the feasts for all time to come; at the beginning of the months in their seasons and holy days in their order for a*

memorial at fixed times, with an offering of the lips I will bless Him as fixed and decreed forever . . .

On Eternal Being mine eye does gaze. Foresight, which is hidden from men of knowledge, and subtle design surpassing the sons of man, the source of justice and store of strength with a fountain of glory unknown to fleshly counsel—To His elect has God granted them for an eternal possession, and has given them an inheritance in the lot of the Holy Ones; and with the Sons of Heaven He has united their council as a conclave in common and council of holy pattern, as an eternal plantation for all time to come.

From the sacred writings of the Testaments of the Twelve Patriarchs, written more than a century before the birth of Jesus, they would have sung praises to the Messiah. For example, from the Testament of Levi we have:

> *And his star shall arise in heaven as of a king.*
>
> *Lighting up the light of knowledge as the sun the day, and he shall be magnified in the world.*
>
> *He shall shine forth as the sun on the earth, and shall remove all darkness from under heaven, and there shall be peace in all the earth.*
>
> *The heavens shall exult in his days, and the earth shall be glad, and the clouds shall rejoice;*
>
> *And the knowledge of the Lord shall be poured forth upon the earth, as the water of the seas.*

And also lines from the Book of the Secrets of Enoch:

> *The giver of light comes to give brightness to the whole world, and the morning guard takes shape, which is the rays of the sun, and the sun of the earth goes out, and receives its*

brightness to light up the whole face of the earth. . . . I have seen the Lord's eyes, shining like the sun's rays and filling the eyes of man with awe.

The Gospel of Matthew records the words of Jesus on this theme:

The light of the body is the eye: if therefore thine eye be single, thy whole body be full of light.

For Enoch had written:

When all creation visible and invisible, as the Lord created it, shall end, then every man goes to the great judgement, and then all time shall perish, and the years, and thenceforward there will he neither months nor days nor hours, they will stuck together and will not be counted.

There will be one aeon, and all the righteous who shall escape the Lord's great judgement, shall be collected in the great aeon, —or the righteous the great aeon will begin, and they trill lire eternally, and then too there will he amongst them neither labour, nor sickness, nor humiliation, nor anxiety, nor need, nor violence, nor night, nor darkness, but great light.

And they shall have a great indestructible wall, and a paradise bright and incorruptible, for all corruptible things shall pass away, and there will be eternal life.

And every person belonging to the Community founded by Jesus and His disciples awaited the coming of the Great Day of the Lord. They faced the rising sun with hopeful attitude, such as that of the author of the Odes of Solomon:

As the sun is the joy to them that seek for its daybreak, so is my joy the Lord;

Because He is my Sun and His rays have lifted me up; and His light hath dispelled all darkness from My face.

In Him I have acquired eyes and have seen His holy day: Ears have become mine and I have heard His truth.

The thought of knowledge hath been thine, and I have been delighted through Him.

The way of error I have left, and have walked towards Him and have received salvation from Him, without grudging.

As the eyes of a son to his father, so are my eyes, O Lord, at all times towards thee.

For with thee are my consolations and my delight.

Turn not away thy mercies from me, O Lord: and take not thy kindness from me.

He hath filled me with words of truth; that I may speak the same:

And like the flow of waters flows truth from my mouth, and my lips show forth His fruit.

And He has caused His knowledge to abound in me, because the mouth of the Lord is the true Word, and the door of His light;

And the Most High hath given it to His words, which are the interpreters of His own beauty, and the repeaters of His praise, and the confessors of His counsel, and the heralds of His thought, and the chasteners of His servants.

For the Swiftness of the Word is inexpressible, and like its expression is its swiftness and force;

And its course knows no limit. Never doth it fail, but it stands sure, and it knows not descent nor the way of it.

For as its work is, so is its end: for it is light and the dawning of thought.

> *And by it the worlds talk one to the other; and in the Word there were those that were silent:*
>
> *And from it came love and concord; and they spake one to the other whatever was theirs, and they were penetrated by the Word,*
>
> *And they knew Him who made them, because they were in concord; for the mouth of the Most High spake to them; and His explanation ran by means of it:*
>
> *For the dwelling-place of the Word is man: and its truth is love.*
>
> *Blessed are they who by means thereof have understood everything, and have known the Lord in His truth.*
>
> *Behold! the Lord is our mirror: open the eyes and see them in Him: and learn the manner of your face.*

A baptismal hymn, quoted in the Epistle to the Ephesians (5:14) and recorded by Clement of Alexandria in his Protreptikos (8:84), was chanted by new Christians:

> *Awake, thou sleeper, rise up from among the dead, and he who is Christ the Lord shall enlighten thee, the sun of resurrection begotten before the dayspring giving life by his beams.*

The identification of Christ with the sun, God's Word manifesting in the heart and center of all light and energy manifesting in the world, is quite common in the ancient writings of the original Christians. This had its roots in the powerful writings of the Essenes who were influenced by teachings outside of Palestine.

9: ANCIENT RELIGIONS AND THE SUN

Solar teachings were also known within the Graeco-Roman world, Egypt, Persia, and other areas that were under the influence of the Indo-European solar religions, all of which stemmed from the original teaching that can be traced to the very beginning of humankind's appearance on the planet. Had the Phoenicians, Greeks, or Romans crossed the oceans to conquer the Americas before the Spaniards and Portuguese (who, under the sway of the Roman Catholic Church, had long since eradicated the solar teachings of antiquity from their doctrines by replacing the sun with Jesus) they would have found doctrines that had the same origin, and differing little from their own, existing among the Mexicans and Peruvians. Such was the universality of the original teachings that found their way into all the world, though each in its own particular way had become paganized and perverted into a nature-worship through which the ruling priesthood propitiated numerous gods, just as had been done in the so-called Old World. The origins of the religions that the Spaniards found go far back to the high cultures that had long since disappeared with the coming of the Aztecs, Maya, and Incas. Be this as it may, baptism, confession of sins and penance, and a ritual of communion were all known in the Americas. The following lines, taken from the writings of Fray Bernardino de Sahagun, a Spanish missionary who recorded many sayings and religious writings of the Nahuas of Mexico, show the spiritual union that existed between the believer and the sun as the suppliant addressed his offerings:

> *I offer, offer flowering cocoa: that I may be sent to the House of the Sun! Beautiful and very rich is the crown of quetzal plumes: may I know the House of the Sun; may I go to that place!*
>
> *Oh, no one contains in his soul the lovely inebriate flower: sparse cocoa flowers giving their fragrance in Huexotzinco's water.*
>
> *Each time the sun climbs this mountain my heart cries and is sad: would it were the flower of my heart: painted in beautiful colours!*
>
> *The King of those who return sings of the flowers! There is flowery intoxication; rejoice at the feast, oh ye princes; there is beautiful dancing: this is the House of Our Father the Sun.*

The following lines, taken from the ancient writings of the Mexicans, were given by the elders to youths entering the colleges. This shows the spiritual education and instruction in ethics given at an early age so children might be literate and wise:

> *Take great pains to make yourselves friends of God who is in all parts, and is invisible and impalpable, and it is proper that you give him all your heart and body, and look that you be not proud in your heart, nor yet despair, nor be cowardly of spirit; but that you be humble in your heart and have hope in God. . . . Be at peace with all, shame yourselves before none and to none be disrespectful; respect all, esteem all, defy no one, for no reason affront any person. . . . Humble yourselves before all*

though they say what they like of you; be silent, and though they bring you as low as they please, answer no word. . . .

Look thou, son, thou shalt not be honoured, nor obeyed and esteemed, but thou shalt be ordered, thou must he humble and despised and cast down; and if thy body gather to itself strength and pride, punish and humble it; look that thou remember not any carnal thing! . . . Look that thou be not surfeited with food, be temperate, love and practice abstinence and fasting. . . . And also, my son, thou must take good care to understand our lord's books; unite thyself with the wise and clever, and those of good understanding.

The words and expressions of the lines quoted above and in those following may appear strange to many versed in the writings of the Judaeo-Christian world, but the spirit in which they were written shows that people everywhere share a common urge to offer oral confession for having committed sins. The following lines are extracts from a sermon given by a confessor to a penitent and clearly demonstrate that the penitent is advised to show sorrow, to repent, and to do penance through a blood sacrifice, as was common to all ancient world religions; and above all, to do good works by helping and giving to the poor after having made bloodless sacrifices of parchment and copal (incense):

Oh brother, . . . thou hast come to a place where snares and nets are tangled and piled one upon another, so that none can pass without falling into them. . . . These are thy sins, which are not only snares and nets and holes into which thou hast fallen, but also wild beasts, that kill and rend the body and the soul. . . . When thou wast created and sent here, thy father and mother Quetzalcoatl made thee like a precious stone. . . . But by thine own will and choosing thou didst become soiled . . . and now thou hast confessed. . . . Thou hast uncovered and made manifest all thy sins to our lord who shelters and purifies all sinners; and take not this as mockery, for in truth thou hast en-

tered the fountain of mercy, which is like the clearest water with which our lord god, who shelters and protects us all, washes away the dirt from the soul. . . . Now thou art born anew; now dost thou begin to live, and even now our lord god gives thee light and a new Sun; now also dost thou begin to flower, and to put forth shoots like a very clean precious stone issuing from thy mother's womb where thou art created. . . . It is fitting that thou do penance, working a year or more in the house of god, and there shalt thou draw blood, and shalt pierce thy body with cactus thorns; and that thou make penance for the adulteries and other filth thou hast done, thou shalt pass osiers [willow sticks] twice a day, one through thine ears and one through thy tongue; and not only as penance for the carnal sins already mentioned, but also for words and injuries with which thou hast affronted and hurt thy neighbours, with thy evil tongue. And for the ingratitude in which thou hast held the favours our lord hast done thee, and for thy inhumanity to thy neighbours in not making offering of the goods bestowed upon thee by god nor in giving to the poor the temporal goods our lord bestowed upon thee. It shall be thy duty to offer parchment and copal, and also to give alms to the needy who starve and who have neither to eat nor drink nor to be clad, though thou know how to deprive thyself of food to give them, and do thy best to clothe those who go naked and in rags; look that their flesh is as thine, and that they are men as thou art.

In addition to the sacrament of public confession and atonement for sins, the Mexicans, as other American peoples, participated in the bloodless sacrifice of the sun god Huitzilopochtli and the communion with the sacred elements that represented the immolated god who was pierced with an arrow; having partaken of the consecrated bread, transubstantiated into the body of the god, the worshiper then partook of immortality: a foretaste of the eternal life which was to be his with the god in heaven:

> *They took seeds of grain and cleaned them well. . . . They ground them carefully, then when the flour was very fine they made dough and with this modelled the body of Huitzilopochtli. Next day a man named Quetzalcoatl shot the body of Huitzilopochtli with an arrow having a stone head, and thrust it into his heart . . . and after having killed him, they broke him in pieces . . . and they took Huitzilopochtli's heart to the lord or King, and all the body and the pieces, which were as the kisses of Huitzilopochtli, they shared in equal parts among the natives of Mexico and Tlatelolco. . . . Thus did they share among them the four parts of the body of Huitzilopochtli. . . . In the districts each person ate a piece of the body of the god.*

This ceremony, practiced in the Americas, has a striking similarity to the Eucharistic meal of the Mithrites, as well as to that of the Christian Church in which the body of Jesus is broken and consumed by the faithful in holy communion, thus partaking of Jesus's divine nature.

Quetzalcoatl, the remarkable prophet and teacher of the Americas, has been compared with Viracocha of Peru and Kukulcan of the Maya by some and thought to be one and the same civilizing agent who brought a spiritual message that included an ethical religion that inspired millions of Indians. His miracles included walking on water, healing the sick, making the blind to see, and all the other signs of a holy man. No human being would have had sufficient understanding to invent the works attributed to him, and we can only assume that Quetzalcoatl, or whatever name he was known by, was a mythico-historical figure as much as was Jesus or any of the better known prophet-teachers. According to legend, Quetzalcoatl, dwelled among the dead for four days, then arose in the sky as Venus, the Morning Star, inhabiting the heavens with the sun. Quetzalcoatl was, then, a savior as were so many others before and after him in different parts of the world; in each case, the teachers brought a similar message. Quetzalcoatl prophesied he would come again to inaugurate a new era on earth that would be announced by the birth of a new sun—the Fifth Sun—that would appear following many earthquakes and cosmic upheavals that would purify the earth and humankind in a consuming fire. From this event the elect of God would arise luminous, reunited with their immortal souls, to return to their Father in the Sun, who is the maker and creator of all, in perpetual communion. It is unfortunate that the once-great religion founded by Quetzalcoatl had degenerated into the pitiful state it was in when the Spaniards, who were themselves adherents of a degenerated Christianity, arrived.

Christianity, which has its roots in the older teachings preserved by the Essenes, may be traced back to the Iranians (Persians), who conquered the Babylonians who were holding the Jews captive and in exile about six hundred years before the coming of Jesus. During their seventy years of exile, the Israelite holy persons were influenced by the solar doctrines of the Iranians' Zoroastrian faith, which included teachings on light and the sun, the immortality of the human soul, the spiritual resurrection of the soul, and eternal life in the world of God. These concepts were absent from the older teachings of the Jews. As Jesus, the divine being, had come down to earth disguised in human form, so had the Iranian *Fravashis* (Light beings) come in mortal bodies in order to fight against the Powers of Darkness and to teach humankind the true doctrines of Light and the transfiguration of the body that was possible through them. The Zoroastrian prophets or reformers, called Saoshyants, were the benefactors of the community come to restore the lost teachings, which included the doctrine of the Amesha-Spenta and the Yazata, the adorable ones, or Angels of God, who inhabited the regions of the light of the Sun; Sraosha, the guardian spirit of humanity, a pure youth who is to come at the final Consummation of the world; and Sraosha's sister, Ashi Vanguhi, the feminine protector of the human race, who will aid humanity in their worship of Ahura Mazda, creator of Immortal Light.

The Zamyad Yasht says: [The Saoshyant] *shall restore the world, which will then never grow old and never die, never decay and never perish, ever live and ever increase, and be master over its wish, when the dead will rise, when life and immortality will come, and the world will be restored at God's wish.*

In the Zoroastrian religion, Mithra, a savior-messenger of the Light, mediator and lord of the dawn, who made his daily rounds on a golden chariot, accompanied by other intelligences, precedes the rising sun. The followers of Mithra gathered on the summits, or stood in the waters, lifting their hands in prayer before the rising sun imploring the spirit of Aredvi Sura Anahita to guard over them and help them in their fight against the Evil One while they sang the divine Songs of Zarathustra (Zoroaster):

And this I ask Thee, O Ahura Mazda! The truthful righteous striving to further the well-being of his house, his province, and his country, How shall he be like unto Thee?

When shall he be worthy of Thee? What actions of his shall most appeal to Thee? Clear is all this to the man of wisdom, as to the man who carefully thinks, he who upholds Truth with all the might of his power, he who upholds Truth to the utmost in his word and deed, he, indeed, is Thy most valued helper, O Mazda Ahura!

To him, who is Thy true friend in spirit and in actions, O Mazda Ahura, to him Thou shalt give Healthful Weal and Immortality; to him Thou shalt give perpetual communion with Truth and the Kingdom of Heaven, and to him Thou shalt give the sustaining strength of the Good Mind.

At eventide, Zoroastrians saluted the setting sun, repenting of their sins and asking for compassion; for as the light of the sun was shed upon the earth in order to sustain life, the Word of God came down to humankind to instruct them in the Holy Way. Though the sacrifice of bulls and goats was part of the older ritual, there was also a bloodless sacrifice (*Yasna*) which was a communion of bread in which the Haoma (the dual god: the physical and the spiritual) was present and was partaken of by the communicants. Fire, like water, was a sacred element that symbolized the presence of God, for fire was likened to a messenger that could carry the prayers of the adherent heavenward. The Zoroastrian religion exceeded Asiatic religions in the degree of advancement in ethical and moral life.

It is interesting to note that the cultivation of corn, which played such a prominent part in the life and religion of Mexico and Peru, was also carried on by the Zoroastrians and identified with righteousness; work and industry were integral parts of the religion, as in the case of the well-organized Inca, Mayan, and Aztec communities, where social life was one of harmonious industry.

Mithra, who had been created from a rock by Ormazd, an event witnessed by shepherds who then brought gifts to the Light child and adored him, drove a fiery chariot through the sky in which he carried the souls of humans to the celestial realms. He was the divine mediator between humans and God, a savior and benefactor of earthly life. He bestowed upon his followers protection, light, beauty, health, long life, material wealth, offspring, sovereignty, and power. The Romans, who were followers of the Unconquerable Sun, were also followers of Mithra. They believed that Mithra's blessings gave them the intelligence to rule the then known world for centuries. Romans saluted the sun in order to sacrifice all that is good to Him: *Hail!*

O Dawn! Hail to Thee! Hail! . . . Hail! Sol Invictus, author of all good, Spirit of beauty, purity, and light. The eternal fire, in which the presence of God was believed to reside, burned perpetually in Rome on Palatine Hill and on the federal altar of Alba Longa.

The Roman regard for the sun and the Intelligence behind it is best illustrated in excerpts from the Emperor Julian's "Hymn to King Helios," the Sun:

> *What I am now about to say I consider to be of the greatest importance for all things "that breathe and move upon the earth" and have a share in existence and a reasoning soul and intelligence, but above all others it is of importance to myself. For I am a follower of Helios Mithrasi. And of this fact I possess within me, known to myself alone, proofs more certain than I can give. But this at least I am permitted to say without sacrilege, that from my childhood an extraordinary longing for the rays of the god penetrated deep into my soul; and from my earliest years my mind was so completely swayed by the light that illumines the heavens that not only did I desire to gaze intently at the sun, but whenever I walked abroad in the night season, when the firmament was clear and cloudless, I abandoned all else without exception and gave myself up to the beauties of the heavens; . . . I envy the good fortune of any man to whom the god has granted to inherit a body built of the seed of holy and inspired ancestors, so that he can unlock the treasures of wisdom; nor do 1 despise that lot with which I was myself endowed by the god Helios, that I should be born of a house that rules and governs the world in my time; but further, I regard this god, if we may believe the wise, as the common father of all mankind. For it is said with truth that man and the sun together beget man, and that the god sows this earth with souls which proceed not from himself alone but from the other gods also; and for what purpose, the souls reveal by the kind of lives that they select. . . .*

> *This divine and wholly beautiful universe, from the highest vault of heaven to the lowest limit of the earth, is held together by the continuous providence of the god, has existed from eternity ungenerated, is imperishable for all time to come, and is guarded immediately by nothing else than the Fifth Substance [quintessence] whose culmination is the beams of the sun; and in the second and higher degree, so to speak, by the intelligible world; but in a still loftier sense it is guarded by the King of the whole universe, who is the center of all things that exist. He, therefore, whether it is right to call him the Supra-Intelligible, or the Idea of Being, and by Being I mean the whole intelligible region, or the One, since the One seems somehow to be prior to all the rest, or, to use Plato's name for him, the Good; at any rate this uncompounded cause of the whole reveals to all existence beauty, and perfection, and oneness, and irresistible power; and in virtue of the primal creative substance that abides in it, produced, as middle among the middle and intellectual, creative causes, Helios the most mighty god, proceeding from itself and in all things like unto itself.*

Similar fires were kept burning in Greece, where Pan (Nature) and Helios (the Sun) were honored at Olympia, Athere Polias, and at Delos, the birthplace of Apollo and Artemis. Everlasting fires were kept burning in all the lands that were influenced by the Indo-Aryan solar religions that spread over Europe, India, and Persia and which, according to the Avesta, divided the world into seven regions. A common doctrine was shared in all these areas, and that is why fires were found on the altars in Germany where Thor was honored, in Prussia where Perkum was honored, in Lithuania where Zinoz was honored, and in the Slavic countries where the God of Light was honored as the firstborn son of God. The Sun and the Sky Father were known in Russia; the Scandinavian countries of Norway, Sweden, and Denmark; and also in France and Italy. In Ireland an eternal fire burned at

Kildare in honor of Bridgit the Bright. In England the sun was honored at the great astronomical sun temple of Stonehenge.

Perpetual fires were also maintained in Peru, in the temples of the Incas. In Peru, Viracocha was the supreme deity or Creator God (Father of all, who did not require sacrifice from humans) and He is not to be confused with Inti, the physical sun. The Virgins of the Sun cultivated corn at the temples of the Royal Cult of the Sun and offered libations to the sacred elements. Even though various names for God were used, there was but one Light, one God, that played an important part in the life and religion of the Children of the Sun who were so far removed and remote from their brothers and sisters in other parts of the world. That the Incas inherited their solar religion from earlier cultures is evidenced by the great Sun Temples at Chavin, Tiahuanaco, Moche, and other parts of the empire.

The Mexican sun priests, like the Incas to the south, prayed to God every morning to send the physical sun, with its light and heat. Oftentimes they used magic to call the sun, which indicates that the sun was a servant to man, not a god as generally understood. Their invocations and morning services were similar to those of the Essenes and the original Christians, who inherited and expanded upon the tradition.

The Egyptians venerated one God of the Sun but used different names for various aspects of it: Ra (Re) was the creator of the universe, the original King of Egypt; Atum was the light of the sun at sunrise; Horus was the light at sunset; Aten represented the physical sun; and Pharaoh was the living Sun God on earth.

The following excerpts are taken from Pharaoh Akhnaten's famous Hymn to the Sun (written about fifteen hundred years before the birth of Jesus) in which we find the first recorded expression of monotheism:

You rise glorious at the heavens' edge, O living Aten!
You in whom all life began.
When you shone from the eastern horizon
You filled every land with your beauty.
You are lovely, great and glittering,
You go high above the lands you have made
Embracing them with your rays
Holding them fast for your beloved son.
Though you are far away, your rays are on earth;
Though you fill men's eyes, your footprints are unseen.

You make the seasons for the sake of your creation,
The winter to cool them, the summer that they may taste your heat.
You have made far skies so that you may shine in them.
Your disk in its solitude looks on all that you have made,
Appearing in its glory and gleaming both near and far.
Out of your singleness you shape a million forms—
Towns and villages, fields, roads and the river.
All eyes behold you, bright Disk of the day.

There is none other who knows you save Akhenaten, your son,
You have given him insight of your purposes.
He understands your power.
All the creatures of the world are in your hand
Just as you have made them.

With your rising they live, with your setting they die.
You yourself are the span of life, men live through you.
Their eyes filled with beauty till the hour of your setting.
All labour is set aside
When you sink in the west.

You established the world for your son,
He who was born of your body,
King of Upper Egypt and Lower Egypt,
Living in Truth, Lord of the Two Lands,
Neferkheprure, Wanre,
The Son of Re, Living in Truth, Lord of Diadems,
Akhenaten great in his length of days.
And for the King's Great Wife,
She whom he loves,
For the Lady of the Two Lands, Nefernefruaten-Nefertiti
May she live and flower forever and ever.

The Hindus also revered the sun, as is indicated by the following Vedic hymn:

Light-giving Varuna, thy piercing glance does scan

In quick succession all this stirring, active world,

Measuring our days and nights, and spying out all creatures.

Surya with flaming locks, clear-sighted god of day,

Thy seven ruddy mares bear on thy rushing car.

... To thy refulgent orb.

Beyond this lower gloom, and upward to the light

Would we ascend, O Sun! Thou god among the gods.

Each morning the Brahmin prays for the sun to rise. Twelve different names for the sun are intoned in the Brahma Purana. The sun was considered to be the divine Vivifier, Surya. In Babylonia, where we find great Temples of the Sun, the mighty Sun God was called Shamash. The Assyrian and Syrian astrologers, famous for their knowledge of the heavens, based their science, which had its origin in the earlier Mesopotamian civilization, on the sun. Their sciences involved the art of developing their eyes to see the sun and the stars in a way not natural for ordinary man. They observed and communed with the heavenly bodies for long periods. To them, the sun was not just a gaseous orb that sent light and heat into the solar system but a living organism that charged humans with a spiritual knowledge that purified their minds, bodies, souls, and spirits. They communicated with the gods from other worlds through heavenly bodies and thereby incorporated their characteristics. It was natural, then, that the ancient astrologers and scientists of that day and age elevated the sun as King of the whole universe, the generator and sustainer of all life on the planet; the ruling power of the world, master and heart of humankind.

To Socrates and the Greek intellectuals, the Sun God was Apollo. Plato called the sun the offspring of the First God; whereas the First God was outside the visible universe, the sun was the son of God, the mediator between humankind and the Creator-Father. The physical sun was considered to be the visible symbol of the spiritual Sun. Greek thinkers believed the sky gods to be supreme: Apollo and Zeus used the sun as a present-day speaker would a microphone to amplify his words when addressing a large audience. The sun was not seen as a god, but as a physical object that could be measured and was not personified or worshiped.

The Roman emperors Constantine and Julian saw the sun as having three aspects: the Sun of the Intelligible World, the Sun of the Intelligent World, and the Sun of the Sensory World. That Constantine saw Christ as a fourth aspect of the Sun is evidenced by his conversion to Christianity after having observed a cross in the sky over the face of the sun following a great victory on the battlefield. Julian believed that Asclepius was this fourth aspect or savior of humankind, as opposed to Helios-Mithra or even Christ. In any event, all saviors were identified with the sun in one form or another.

The Jewish religion was involved with the sun, as we know from previous pages describing the Essenes and Therapeutae. The Lord commanded Moses to keep a perpetual fire burning on the altar; its flame was to be replenished each morning by the priests so that it would never go out. The Angel of the Lord appeared to Moses in a flame of fire, out of the midst of a bush (Ex. 3:2), and the Lord spoke to Moses using the fire as an intermediary force. Reverence for the sun became one of the aspects of ritual permitted in Jerusalem, one such place being called Beth-shemesh, the House of the Sun, in Judah. The sun was not personified, nor was the physical sun worshiped, since it was only a visible representation of the invisible God, as was the fire through which the Lord spoke to Moses. We are reminded of this fact from the writings of the Old Testament where the coming deliverer was spoken of as the Sun of Righteousness, God's Light, the primordial, or First, Sun, that would shine again on all humankind.

10: THE NEW BIRTH

Jesus succeeded Mithra and all the other agencies of God known in the ancient world. He came as the visible Christ, a messenger from God to humanity, exemplifying and announcing the Light and grace given by God. All the great solar religions had awaited a savior or Messiah, and Jesus's self-proclaimed message, authenticated by cosmic events, gave Him a living authority that superseded that of the ancient saviors. Following His spiritual resurrection, He spoke through the agency of the Sun, wherein was found God's Word, the Logos, transmitted in love, understanding, and wisdom. The great ethical religion that was dynamically founded by His disciples inspired the minds of people everywhere.

Jesus's original followers traveled throughout the ancient world, taking the Gospel of Christ to those found worthy to hear. Men and women in all walks of life were illuminated by the spirit of Christ, all intent upon establishing the Kingdom of God on earth forever. The ways of human tradition were cast aside, and those reborn in the Word of God lived afresh, glorified in a new body of Light, a new mind, and a Christ-like spirit. Greeks, Jews, Romans, Persians, Egyptians—men and women of all races, colors, nationalities, and creeds: barbarians, intellectuals, slaves, free people, rich, and poor—all joined in a universal fellowship, one nation under Christ, a new people, each measured by the Light of self-salvation through God and not by social standards or wealth, title, position, or rank. Each put on the garments of righteousness and eternal life and glory, all being members of the Messianic Body as one family with God at its head. What had been lost after the fall of Adam and Eve was being restored. It was now possible for humans to walk in universal fellowship with God as they had in the beginning of the creation.

The prophets prayed for the Word of God to come into the world and to restore what had been lost—the complete communion between God and His lost children. The message brought by Jesus promised such a new state. Indeed, Jesus and His disciples taught that the establishment of God's Kingdom on earth could only come about through a change in humankind's very being.

Before this could transpire, the old world had to come to an end. This concept of "an end" brought people of all faiths together into one community. They withdrew from the affairs of the world, disdaining civic responsibilities, participation in military service, and the Roman patriotism of the day, which called for swearing allegiance to the emperor and sacrificing to the popular gods of the old religions. Even marriage and the procreation of children was rejected as it only tended to prolong the agonies of the world of flesh with all its desires that resulted in suffering and eventual death.

Members of the new society, who came to be known by the popular masses as Christians, banded together in a spiritual way of life. Master and slave, man and woman labored together in universal fellowship bent on ushering in a new age under the Supreme God. They needed no temples as did other religious societies. Theirs was a secret, mystic order that lived apart from the world, refusing to accept the demands of the civil authorities with their unjust laws that only furthered the state at the expense of the individual living under God's ordinances. They sought the salvation of the human soul and the transformation of the material world into a spiritual reality. Their acceptance of celibacy was intended to extinguish the fleshly human species. While this concept appalled the Roman authorities, Christians believed it to be the only way for individuals to help God restore the world to what it had originally been before the Fall.

Conflict with the state was inevitable, for if the Christians had their way, the entire structure of society would be imperiled and possibly lead to civil disorder. The final result would be the end of the world as people knew it. Therefore, the state persecuted them for the common good. The hostility began with the crucifixion of Jesus and the death of His disciples. Persecution continued through the third century and did not end until the beginning of the fourth century. By this time the destruction of the original Christian teachings was complete. With the marriage of the Church to the state, the purely spiritual goals of the former faded. What had been a secret society of relatively few dedicated souls was changed into a popular Church for the masses of society. Christianity became a servant of the state. Its members participated in civic affairs, joined the army, and, in general, became good citizens. It was Rome, then, that gave birth to popular Christianity as we know it today.

Even though many religions of the world prior to the coming of Jesus had embraced the sun, He had announced something that had not been available to humankind before. This was the one great, unfulfilled promise of all the solar religions: the promise of the Word of God coming forth to humankind out of a spiritual Sun. As God spoke to the prophets through the medium of fire, He would speak to humankind through this new Sun. Therefore, the physical sun would be secondary to God's Sun. Jesus was not delivering philosophical or theological discourses representative of a new attitude or a new religion (of which the ancient world had more than enough). He was more than an interpreter of divine teachings and Law. His coming was divinely inspired, and His teachings were divine concepts germinated in the Consciousness of God. A new dimension was added to religion. Jesus had announced: *I am come to send fire on earth.* Paul mentions the eternal element in his First Epistle to the Corinthians:

> *Every man's work shall be made manifest: for the day shall declare it, because it shall be revealed by fire; and the fire shall try every man's work of what sort it is.*
>
> *If any man's work abide which he hath built thereupon, he shall receive a reward,*
>
> *If any man's work shall be burned, he shall suffer loss: but he himself shall be saved; yet so as by fire.*
>
> *Know ye not that ye are the temple of God, and that the Spirit of God dwelleth in you?*
>
> *If any man defile the temple of God, him shall God destroy; for the temple of God is holy, which temple ye are.*
>
> *Let no man deceive himself, If any man among you seemeth to be wise in this world, let him become a fool, that he may be wise,*
>
> *For the wisdom of this world is foolishness with God. For it is written, He taketh the wise in their own craftiness.*

The words of Enoch proclaim the relationship of God with fire in chapter 33 of the Secrets of Enoch:

> *And for all the heavenly troops I imaged the image and essence of fire, and my eye looked at the very hard, firm rock, and from the gleam of my eye the lightning received its wonderful nature,*

which is both fire in water and water in fire, and one does not put out the other, nor does the one dry up the other, therefore the lightning is brighter than the sun, softer than water and firmer than hard rock.

And from the rock I cut off a great fire, and from the fire I created the orders of the incorporeal ten troops of angels, and their weapons are fiery and their raiment a burning flame, and I commanded that each one should stand in his order.

It is evident from these passages that God used the media of light and fire to speak to prophets, holy persons, and visionaries. Joseph dreamed of the sun and the moon and the eleven stars (Gen. 37:9); and Joshua made the sun and the moon stand still following his victory over the Amorites when he spoke to the Lord (Jos. 10:12–14). Psalms 84:11 declares that the Lord God is a *sun and shield*. Therefore, no God-fearing person, no prophet nor holy man would worship the sun anymore than he would worship any natural thing created by God; but it is certain that the Sun is, or can be, an intermediary by which humans can communicate with God and by which God can communicate with them.

The apocryphal Two Books of Jeu in the Gnostic writings has five of the Apostles speaking to Jesus:

Lord Jesus, thou living one, whose goodness is spread abroad upon those who have found his wisdom and his form, in which he shines—O Light, that is in the light which has illumined our heart until we received the light of life—O true word, which through knowledge teaches us the hidden knowledge of the Lord Jesus, the living one. Jesus, the living one, answered and said, Blessed is the man who knoweth this, and has brought the heaven down, and carried the earth and sent it to heaven, and he became the Midst, for it is nothing. The apostles answered, saying: Jesus, thou living one, O Lord, explain to us in what way

> *one may bring down the heaven, for we have followed thee, that thou might teach us the true light.*

We learn from these lines that there is a Light within the bright light of Jesus; the Word, or divine knowledge, transmitted by the spirit of Jesus, just as the greater Light of God manifested to Paul on the road to Damascus through the light of the midday sun. While there is the Light of God's word manifest in Jesus, it is always accompanied by the light appearance of the body of Jesus. Thus there is always an interrelationship between matter and spirit. We also learn from the ensuing words that the doctrines of Jesus were secret and not intended for everyone. These doctrines were available to persons qualified through proper initiation and were always to be transmitted in a secret formula, orally and in written form, consisting of the obscure language of the apocalyptic tradition, to those able to understand and comply with the requirements of the fellowship, which were total dedication and commitment:

> *These mysteries which I shall give you, preserve, and give them to no man except he be worthy of them. Give them not to father nor to mother, to brother or to sister or to kinsman, neither for food nor for drink, nor for woman-kind, neither for gold nor for silver, nor for anything at all of this world. Preserve them, and give them to no one whatsoever for the sake of the good of this whole world.*

The birth of the new world expected by the disciples failed to materialize, not because Christianity as instituted by Jesus was found wanting, but because the civil authorities of Rome, Israel and, other Mediterranean countries refused to extend religious freedom to the first Christians. This resulted in the total collapse of the community and the eventual perversion of the teachings. What had begun as a spiritual order, dedicated to the overthrow of the old world and the establishment of a new world under God, degenerated into another social religion under a new name. Thus God's New Sun— which could have altered the world— never materialized to humanity, not because it didn't exist, but because humans failed to develop the spiritual attributes necessary to perceive it. It was as if the light had gone out and everything was as it had been before the coming of Jesus. The event was a reenactment of the original act that had taken place in the symbolical Garden of Eden with Adam and Eve, the archetypal Man and Woman. Again, humanity turned away from their Creator, seeking the ways of the material world over the spiritual world, having been led astray by the necessities of the Roman state that emphasized social law and order. As Jesus had warned: *Except your righteousness shall exceed the righteousness of the scribes and Pharisees, ye shall in no case enter the Kingdom of heaven.* Humankind was enmeshed in the law, losing sight of the power of the spirit with its higher standard of laws that could lead them back into the life God had intended for them.

The popular Christian state religion that followed was described by one of the greatest Latin Fathers of the Roman Church, Augustine (345 CE): *That which is now called the Christian religion was not wanting among the ancients from the beginning of the human race, until Christ came in the flesh, after which time the true religion, which already existed, began to be called "Christian."* He later retracted these words, but he was fully aware of the antiquity of the teachings absorbed by the Roman Church that was now called Christian.

Jesus came into the world as a messenger of God, announcing the existence of God's redeeming force. Humankind had only to accept it and apply the system He taught, which was designed to bring about the establishment of a New Age under the direct rulership of God. The final result was to be the end of the world as people knew it (just as the Romans suspected) and the restoration of a World of Light in which people would again regain their stature as creatures of Light, immortal and chosen of God.

This teaching was far grander than anything the Jews under the Mosaic Law could ever suspect, though their prophets had spoken of it in the Holy Scripture they so dearly cherished, as Jesus was so careful to point out. Jesus taught of a spiritual kingdom, not an earthly one; therefore, He failed to fulfill the expectations of the Jewish Messiah who would free the Jews from their enslavement to the Romans. In this respect, Jesus was a Servant of God come to announce the Good News. Never at any time did the original disciples worship Jesus as God.

The deification of Jesus came at a later date. He became the Kyrios (Lord), the personal savior of the masses, replacing the old salvation gods thousands of years old. Instead of adhering to the supreme religious teachings laid down by Jesus, a cult of worship and ritual sprang up around him. Jesus became the sacrifice for humanity's sins. It was His blood that washed them clean. The pagan religions formed a single Catholic faith at Rome and were regenerated under the banner of a solitary savior, Jesus, who took the place of a score of deities. He became the divine offering, the sacrificial victim who took away the sorrows and sins of a needful humanity, bearing them away to a world beyond the grave that they could not enter. The offering of a scapegoat was common at Rome, Greece, and elsewhere in the lands of the Gentiles, where every spring a man was crowned with holy branches, dressed in skins, beaten with rods, and led through the streets carrying the evils of the populace. His death, usually by stoning, assured favorable crops and abundant livestock. Thus the followers of the new religion found a perpetual redeemer in Jesus—the sacrificial lamb.

State Christianity elevated Jesus to the position held by many of the gods, namely, the solar redeemer. Indeed, Christians saw Jesus as the synthesis of the solar deities of the East because they were salvation gods of light, truth, and justice. To Christians, Jesus was the Unconquered Sun who had risen and who reigned in heaven above. December 25 of the Roman calendar (previously celebrated as the rebirth of Mithra and the Unconquered Sun, or Natalis Solis Invicti), the third day after the winter solstice, when the sun began anew its northward journey, was chosen as the birthday of Jesus. Throughout the empire this date was honored as the day when the Heavenly Sky Virgin (the constellation Virgo, rising in the east on that day) conceived and gave birth to the sun, represented by the image of an infant in the shrines of Syria and Egypt. Augustine admonished Christians not to celebrate this day on account of the sun but because of the birth of Christ who had made the sun. The greater number of Christian celebrations were adapted from the ancient religions. The death and resurrection of Attis (celebrated in Rome on March 25, at the beginning of the new astrological year when the sun moved into the sign Aries) was chosen as the day of Jesus's death. Many old dates were adapted by the Church to help convert people of divergent faiths to the one universal faith. Indeed, the Church was accused of imitating the old ways under a new name. The Christian calendar paralleled the old sun cults, running side by side with the cycle of the sun. Sunday (*dies solis*) was the day of the sun at Rome, and while no scriptural passage fixes the day of the resurrection, Sunday was recognized as that day and named as the holy day of the Christian week, supplanting the Sabbath, the sixth and most revered day of the Jews. In short, Jesus became the Sun god: the source of all physical light, the Sun of Justice and the Sun of Righteousness—the image of God. Christian solar imagery replaced that of the old solar cults, and Jesus, the Light being, displaced the sun gods of antiquity—those gods of salvation who fought against darkness: *I am the light of the world: he that followeth me shall not walk in darkness, but shall have the light of life* (John 8:12).

Thus Christianity became a syncretistic religion. Without this assimilation of paganism, there would have been no Christianity as the world knows it today. Though Christianity filled the void left by the decline of the old-world religions, the original message of Jesus, who envisioned the redemption of humankind from the physical cosmos through the redeeming power of God, was lost. Many of His teachings were locked up in the scriptural texts and oral traditions left by the original disciples who had known Jesus. The proper interpretations, however, were lost with the death of those original disciples, who had been schooled in the secret teachings.

It must be accepted, or at least considered, by the reader, that the evangelical writers, who put to writing the message of the Gospel that had been given to them directly by Jesus or His immediate disciples, were in possession of spiritual faculties and a Christ Consciousness in addition to the normal human faculties of cognition and emotion. It was utterly impossible for the average person lacking these spiritual attributes to conceive of what the Gospel writers meant by their cryptic symbology. It was equally impossible for the Gospel writers to describe the teachings, much less the benefits, in everyday language so that others could understand what they wanted to convey. It was something beyond the rational mind, the thinking processes, but did not exclude them.

Fundamental in this teaching was the idea that the evangelists were in possession of the proper means of teaching every human being how to achieve a second birth. They taught that the means, or the way, had been given by Jesus, the divine Word of God incarnate. Jesus was the firstborn, the divine reason emanating from God the Father, come to announce the appearance of a new cycle of God's grace given for the benefit of the human family.

Humankind was imprisoned in the material world: their spirits were asleep, and they could not be freed through their own efforts by means of any human knowledge gained by reason or experience of the mind or senses. The old-world religions, not unfamiliar with this idea, had produced some of the greatest minds and rulers of the time, who found it difficult to let go of their own ideas and accept the idea that Jesus, come from a distant, foreign soil, could possibly be the Messiah or Christ. Because of this problem, the evangelists wrote for a global audience, taking into consideration the known theologies of the day and speaking in a language that could be recognized and understood by those trained in the tenets of sophisticated philosophies. Having attained the second birth, and being therefore in possession of the gnosis, or divine knowledge, the evangelists wrote in defense of their faith, emphasizing the reality of this birth over mere theory or philosophical concepts. Their terminology is not always clear to the untrained.

The divine Word, or Logos, also known as the solar *spermatikos*, or seminal Light, was able to impregnate the human spirit and produce a new person, a spiritual child who took on the image and likeness of God. Mary, the mother of Jesus, had experienced such a conception inasmuch as the seminal Light had impregnated her being. Though her womb had conceived the human child Jesus from her union with Joseph, His earthly father, the higher, spiritual, or Light body and divine nature of Jesus had been conceived by God, and thus Jesus became the first son, or offspring of God, the Word made flesh. The secret Gospel was actually a process whereby the individual was reborn, becoming a second child of God, immortal and divine. Here was an idea to stagger the mind of the normal person. Minds exposed to the simple ethical and moral concepts of religion or the Law of Moses were overwhelmed by this message.

In view of what has been said, it is understandable why the evangelists used symbols and formulas to express their views (much the same as would mathematicians when calculating numbers dealing in millions or billions—the mind cannot process more than it can conceive of anymore than the average intelligence can understand something with which it has no experience). Evangelists writing about the ultradimensional level of existence (a state or condition beyond measurable time and space as ordinary human beings know it, but which is known to Beings of Light) had to resort to symbols when expressing their experience with that state and Christ's system by which it could be attained. Later (by which time the oral teachings that could have helped them understand had been lost) when scholars, intellectuals, theologians, and clergy examined the manuscripts, scrolls, and fragments of the original writings, the encoded message was beyond their comprehension. The ethics and morals of the teachings they could grasp, and that is what came down to the masses and was called Christianity: a socio-religious system. As for the higher benefits that could be realized by application of Christ's system, these remained as distant from human possession as the stars.

The solar religions of antiquity had recognized that all life on the planet evolved in the light and heat of the sun: without it, no life could exist. That is why they looked upon the sun as the begetter of life, which, from a material point of view, it can be considered to be; however, the sophisticated civilizations that developed out of the ancient world, such as those in Persia, Egypt, Greece, Central Europe, Rome, India, Mexico, Peru, and elsewhere, recognized a creative intelligence behind the sun that sustained life and thought. This intelligence they called God. They saw the sun not as a gigantic ball of fire but as a living organism, a star that not only affected all life-forms but was also affected by them. Above all, they saw the physical sun as the generation of an invisible, spiritual sun: Sol Invictus, the Father in Heaven, who existed beyond the visible universe and was humankind's creator. If God were angered, or if humanity lived out of harmony with the sun, the sun would grow old and negate, destroying the earth in a final conflagration. (Nuclear physics recognizes this eventuality, though it predicts this will not occur for several million years.) The ancient prophets had predicted that in the final days of the earth, God's Sun of Righteousness would appear in the heavens sending forth an intense spiritual Light into the world. This invisible Light, not perceived by the physical senses, would affect all living things through the medium of sunlight, the carrier of intelligence, showing the unity of the visible and the invisible and the dependence of the former upon the Creative Intelligence that is the creator of all phenomena, visible and invisible.

The relationship of Jesus to the sun and the intelligence or power transmitted by sunlight is illustrated in the Gospel of Mark regarding the crucifixion of Jesus (15:33–34):

> *And when the sixth hour [noon] was come, there was darkness over the whole land until the ninth hour [3 p.m.]. And at the ninth hour Jesus cried with a loud voice, saying, Eloi, Eloi, lama sabachthani? which is being interpreted, My God, my God, why hast thou forsaken me?*

The passage indicates that Jesus was linked to the sun and to the Light therein. With His impending death, the sun dimmed and upon his death went out, as if God had withdrawn the Light of His Word from the world due to the suffering and death of His Christ. Being related to the Light, Jesus saw the darkening of the sun as a separation from God. The episode is graphically described in the apocryphal Gospel of Peter:

> *Now it was midday and a darkness covered all Judaea. And they became anxious and uneasy lest the sun had already set, since*

he was still alive. For it stands written for them: the sun should not set on one that has been put to death. And one of them said, "Give him to drink gall with vinegar." And they mixed it and gave him to drink. And they fulfilled all things and completed the measure of their sins on their head. And many went about with lamps, and as they supposed that it was night, and they stumbled about. And the Lord called out and cried, "My power, O power, thou hast forsaken me!" And having said this he was taken up. And at the same hour the veil of the temple in Jerusalem was rent in two.

And then the Jews drew the nails from the hands of the Lord and laid him on the earth. And the whole earth shook and there came a great fear. Then the sun shone again, and it was found to be the ninth hour.

This account has Jesus crying out, *My Power, O Power, thou hast forsaken me,* meaning that the source of His power was taken away by the fading of the sun. This passage illustrates Jesus's dependence upon the Light of God the Father and explains why light played such a dominant part in His ministry. The Sun of Jesus transcended the material sun that sends light, warmth, heat, and life to earth. His was a higher, archetypal Sun of Righteousness, God's redeeming divine Light, the generative life-begetting power beyond the visible cosmic order that impregnates the souls of human beings, gives birth to and sustains their immortal spirits. When Jesus lifted His eyes to the sun, He saw not only the material light of nature but the Light of heaven within it, which is only seen with the Light-bearing eyes of the soul.

Herein is the key to the mystery of the living Gospel.

Paul, in his letters to the Thessalonians, reminds the followers of Jesus that the Gospel is not one written with words but of the living spirit and that the Second Coming of Christ is the essential teaching. In his first letter to them (1:5; 5:1–6), he writes:

> *For our gospel came not unto you in word only, but also in power, and in the Holy Ghost. . . . But of the times and the seasons, brethren, ye have no need that I write unto you. For yourselves know perfectly that the day of the Lord so cometh as a thief in the night. For when they shall say, Peace and safety, then sudden destruction cometh upon them, as travail upon a woman with child; and they shall not escape. But ye, brethren, are not in darkness, that that day should overtake you as a thief. Ye are all the children of light, and the children of the day: we are not of the night, nor of the darkness. Therefore let us not sleep, as do others; but let us watch and be sober. . . . Therefore, brethren, stand fast, and hold the traditions which ye have been taught, whether by word, or our epistle. Now our Lord Jesus Christ himself and God, even our Father, which hath loved us, and hath given us everlasting consolation and good hope through grace, Comfort your hearts, and stablish you in every good word and work.*

Paul acknowledged the sufferings of the Gentile Churches in the opening lines of his second Epistle to the Thessalonians (1:3–11):

> *We are bound to thank God always for you, brethren, as it is meet, because that your faith groweth exceedingly, and the charity of every one of you all toward each other aboundeth;*

> *So that we ourselves glory in you in the churches of God for your patience and faith in all your persecutions and tribulations that ye endure:*

> *Which is a manifest token of the righteous judgment of God, that ye may be counted worthy of the kingdom of God, for which ye also suffer:*

> *Seeing it is a righteous thing with God to recompense tribulation to them that trouble you;*

> *And to you who are troubled rest with us, when the Lord Jesus shall be revealed from heaven with his mighty angels,*
>
> *In flaming fire taking vengeance on them that know not God, and that obey not the gospel of our Lord Jesus Christ:*
>
> *Who shall be punished with everlasting destruction from the presence of the Lord, and from the glory of his power;*
>
> *When he shall come to be glorified in his saints, and to be admired in all them that believe (because our testimony among you was believed) in that day.*
>
> *Wherefore also we pray always for you, that our God would count you worthy of this calling, and fulfil all the good pleasure of his goodness, and the work of faith with power.*

He had previously written to them of the persecutions of the Church in Judaea in his first epistle (2:13–20):

> *For this cause also thank we God without ceasing, because, when ye received the word of God which ye heard of us, ye received it not as the word of men, but as it is in truth, the word of God, which effectually worketh also in you that believe.*
>
> *For ye, brethren, became followers of the churches of God which in Judaea are in Christ Jesus: for ye also have suffered like things of your own countrymen, even as they have of the Jews:*
>
> *Who both killed the Lord Jesus, and their own prophets, and have persecuted us; and they please not God, and are contrary to all men:*
>
> *Forbidding us to speak to the Gentiles that they might be saved, to fill up their sins alway: for wrath is come upon them to the uttermost.*

> *But we, brethren, being taken from you for a short time in presence, not in heart, endeavoured the more abundantly to see your face with great desire.*
>
> *Wherefore we would have come unto you, even I, Paul, once and again; but Satan hindered us.*
>
> *For what is our hope, or joy, or crown of rejoicing? Are not even ye in the presence of our Lord Jesus Christ at his coming?*
>
> *For ye are our glory and joy.*

And Paul emphasized the great Day of Christ that would come. Yet, in his Second Epistle to the Thessalonians (2:1–14) he pointed out that before this day would dawn, there would first be a falling away in the Churches, and the world would be under great darkness, the beginnings of which were already at work:

> *Now we beseech you, brethren, by the coming of our Lord Jesus Christ, and by our gathering together unto him,*
>
> *That ye be not soon shaken in mind, or be troubled, neither by spirit, nor by word, nor by letter as from us, as that the day of Christ is at hand.*
>
> *Let no man deceive you by any means: for that day shall not come, except there come a falling away first, and that man of sin be revealed, the son of perdition;*
>
> *Who opposeth and exalteth himself above all that is called God, or that is worshipped; so that he as God sitteth in the temple of God, shewing himself that he is God.*
>
> *Remember ye not, that, when I was yet with you, I told you these things?*
>
> *And now ye know what withholdeth that he might be revealed in his time.*

For the mystery of iniquity doth already work: only he who now letteth will let, until he be taken out of the way.

And then shall that Wicked be revealed, whom the Lord shall consume with the spirit of his mouth, and shall destroy with the brightness of his coming:

Even him, whose coming is after the working of Satan with all power and signs and lying wonders,

And with all deceivableness of unrighteousness in them that perish; because they received not the love of the truth, that they might be saved,

And for this cause God shall send them strong delusion, that they should believe a lie:

That they all might be damned who believed not the truth, but had pleasure in unrighteousness,

But we are bound to give thanks alway to God for you, brethren beloved of the Lord, because God hath from the beginning chosen you to salvation through sanctification of the Spirit and belief of the truth:

Whereunto he called you by our gospel, to the obtaining of the glory of our Lord Jesus Christ.

The apostasy destined to befall the world before the coming of Christ again is graphically illustrated in the New Testament Second Epistle to Timothy (3:1–17; 4:1–5):

This know also, that in the last days perilous times shall come.

For men shall be lovers of their own selves, covetous, boasters, proud, blasphemers, disobedient to parents, unthankful, unholy,

Without natural affection, truce-breakers, false accusers, incontinent, fierce, despisers of those that are good,

Traitors, heady, highminded, lovers of pleasures more than lovers of God;

Having a form of godliness, but denying the power thereof: from such turn away.

For of this sort are they which creep into houses, and lead captive silly women laden with sins, led away with divers lusts,

Ever learning, and never able to come to the knowledge of the truth.

Now as Jannes and Jambres withstood Moses, so do these also resist the truth: men of corrupt minds, reprobate concerning the faith.

But they shall proceed no further: for their folly shall be manifest unto all men, as theirs also was.

But thou hast fully known my doctrine, manner of life, purpose, faith, longsuffering, charity, patience,

Persecutions, afflictions, which came unto me at Antioch, at Iconium, at Lystra; what persecutions I endured: but out of them all the Lord delivered me.

Yea and all that will live godly in Christ Jesus shall suffer persecution.

But till men and seducers shall wax worse and worse, deceiving, and being deceived,

But continue thou in the things which thou hast learned and hast been assured of, knowing of whom thou hast learned them;

And that from a child thou hast known the holy scriptures, which are able to make thee wise unto salvation through faith which is in Christ Jesus.

All scripture is given by inspiration of God, and is profitable for doctrine, for reproof, for correction, for instruction in righteousness:

> That the man of God may be perfect, throughly furnished unto all good works.
>
> I charge thee therefore before God, and the Lord Jesus Christ, who shall judge the quick and the dead at his appearing and his kingdom;
>
> Preach the word; be instant in season, out of season; reprove, rebuke, exhort with all longsuffering and doctrine.
>
> For the time will come when they will not endure sound doctrine; but after their own lusts shall they heap to themselves teachers, having itching ears;
>
> And they shall turn away their ears from the truth, and shall be turned unto fables.
>
> But watch thou in all things, endure afflictions, do the work of an evangelist, make full proof of thy ministry.

Peter carried on the traditional teaching in his Second Epistle (3:1–13):

> This second epistle, beloved, I now I write unto you; in both which I stir up your pure minds by way of remembrance:
>
> That ye may be mindful of the words which were spoken before by the holy prophets, and of the commandment of us the apostles of the Lord and Saviour:
>
> Knowing this first, that there shall come in the last days scoffers, walking after their own lusts,
>
> And saying, Where is the promise of his coming? for since the fathers fell asleep, all things continue as they were from the beginning of the creation.
>
> For this they willingly are ignorant of that by the word of God the heavens were of old, and the earth standing out of the water

and in the water:

Whereby this world that then was, being overflowed with water, perished.

But the heavens and the earth, which are now, by the same word are kept in store, reserved unto fire against the day of judgment and perdition of ungodly men.

But, beloved, be not ignorant of this one thing, that one day is with the Lord as a thousand years, and a thousand years as one day.

The Lord is not slack concerning his promise, as some men count slackness; but is longsuffering to us-ward, not willing that any should perish, but that all should come to repentance.

But the day of the Lord will come as a thief in the night; in the which the heavens shall pass away with a great noise, and the elements shall melt with fervent heat, the earth also and the works that are therein shall be burned up.

Seeing then that all these things shall be dissolved, what manner of persons ought ye to be in all holy conversation and godliness,

Looking for and hasting unto the coming of the day of God, wherein the heavens being on fire shall be dissolved, and the elements shall melt with fervent heat?

Nevertheless we, according to his promise, look for new heavens and a new earth, wherein dwelleth righteousness.

We learn from these words that the great event was to be some time in coming; that the teachings and Christ's ministry were only half accomplished. The Second Coming was an essential part of the message, one which would regenerate and fulfill the original Christian tradition and eventually bring about a World of Light under God. As Christianity fulfilled the old Law, the Second Coming would inaugurate a new teaching that would fulfill the Christian teachings. Jesus makes this distinction clear in a parable recorded in the Gospel of Luke (5:36):

> *No man putteth a piece of a new garment upon an old; if otherwise, then both the new maketh a rent, and the piece that was taken out of the new agreeth not with the old. And no man putteth new wine into old bottles; else the new wine will burst the bottles, and be spilled, and the bottles shall perish. But new wine must be put into new bottles; and both are preserved. No man also having drunk old wine straightway desireth new; for he saith, The old is better.*

No further revelation as recorded in the Bible is possible until Christ shall come a second time to authorize and oversee the teaching. Peter enlightens us on this possibility (2 Peter 1:19–21):

> *We have also a more sure word of prophecy; whereunto ye do well that ye take heed, as unto a light that shineth in a dark place; until the day dawn, and the day star arise in your hearts; Knowing this first, that no prophecy of the scripture is of any private interpretation. For the prophecy came not in old time by the will of man; but holy men of God spoke as they were moved by the Holy Ghost.*

We learn from these lines that the original concepts instituted by Jesus were not to be restored to the Christian Community until Christ's Second Coming and the New Advent of the Church, which would be a new teaching to fulfill the old. It was to be separate, yet related, as were Christianity and Judaism; its only purpose to be the re-establishment of human fellowship with God. It would be directly authorized by Christ, and its prophets would be moved by the Holy Spirit, as was done in olden times.

The Second Coming of Christ is to occur in the latter days, at a time when Christian communities are laboring under apostasy.

We might ask ourselves: what form will Christ assume in the Second Coming? The scriptures tell us that God's Light shall shine sevenfold strong in the last and final days—a Messianic Sun of Righteousness with healing in its rays:

> *Moreover the light of the moon shall be as the light of the sun, and the light of the sun shall be sevenfold, as the light of seven days, in the day that the Lord bindeth up the breach of his people, and healeth the stroke of their wound.* (Isaiah 30:26)

> *The sun shall be no more thy light by day; neither for brightness shall the moon give light unto thee: but the Lord shall be unto thee an everlasting light, and thy God thy glory.*

> *Thy sun shall no more go down; neither shall thy moon withdraw itself for the Lord shall be thine everlasting light, and the days of thy mourning shall be ended.* (Isaiah 60:19–20)

The Light within God's Sun shall nourish the spiritual nature of humankind, serving as divine food. This Light shall burn the souls of people, and they shall yearn for spiritual guidance; for even though they be engaged in material pursuits, their spirits shall hear the Word spoken by God.

The universal Messiah is to be none other than the Light of God, instead of a man-savior whom men can judge and possibly harm, as they have done in the past. Therefore, the true worshipper of God will need no material temple or church as before but will, as a human being, be able to participate spiritually in God's redeeming salvation.

We read in First Corinthians (3:13–19):

> *Every man's work shall be made manifest: for the day shall declare it, because it shall be revealed by fire; and the fire shall try every man's work of what sort it is. If any man's work abide*

which he hath built thereupon, he shall receive a reward. If any man's work shall be burned, he shall suffer loss: but he himself shall be saved; yet so as by fire. Know ye not that ye are the temple of God, and that the Spirit of God dwelleth in you? If any man defile the temple of God, him shall God destroy; for the temple of God is holy, which temple ye are. Let no man deceive himself. If any man among you seemeth to be wise in this world, let him become a fool, that he may be wise. For the wisdom of this world is foolishness with God. For it is written, He taketh the wise in their own craftiness.

The Jewish prophets, having been inspired by Jesus called Christ, bestowed upon the Gentile World the new revelations that fortified and fulfilled the older teachings, not only of Judaism, but also of other religions of the ancient world which had been inspired by the Word (sometimes called the Logos or divine Reason by ancient philosophers). These revelations that grew into the Christian religion could be traced to the beginning, where God is the divine fountain of Light. The author of the Epistle to the Ephesians wrote clearly of the universality of the teachings that were shared with the Gentile nations (3:2–7):

If ye have heard of the dispensation of the grace of God which is given me to you-ward:

How that by revelation he made known unto me the mystery; (as I wrote afore in few words,

Whereby, when ye read, ye may understand my knowledge in the mystery of Christ)

Which in other ages was not made known unto the sons of men, as it is now revealed unto his holy apostles and prophets by the Spirit;

That the Gentiles should be fellow heirs, and of the same body, and partakers of his promise in Christ by the gospel:

> *Whereof I was made a minister, according to the gift of the grace of God given unto me by the effectual working of his power.*

Since the Gentile peoples inherited the Christian revelation, it is evident that the new Revealer, the holder of the office of Christ in the Second Advent of the Christian Community, will emerge from the Gentiles to proclaim the Great Day of the Lord. Though new, the Messenger of God will be linked to the earlier holder of the office of Christ.

Many ancient texts refer to a twin-savior. One of these texts, the Pistis Sophia, mentions the Child of the Child, a mystery that has intrigued scholars over the centuries. What is meant by the expression *Child of the Child*, twin-savior? In the Apocryphon, or Secret Book, of John, an early Gnostic document in the Coptic language, we find the following lines:

> *There are the four lights which stand by the Self-generator of the gods, the twelve Aeons, which stand by the Child, by the great Self-generator-Christ, through the good pleasure of God, the Invisible Spirit. The twelve Aeons belong to the son, the Self-generated.*

The Birth in the Cave, found in the Latin Infancy Gospel in the Arundel Manuscript, purportedly recording the midwife's account, contains the following lines:

> *When therefore the hour drew nearer, the might of God manifested itself. And the maiden (Mary) stood looking up to heaven, and became as a grape divine. For now the end of the events of salvation was far advanced. And when the light had come forth, Mary worshipped him whom she saw that she had brought forth. And the child himself shone brightly round about like the sun, and was pure and most beautiful to behold, since he alone appeared as peace spreading peace everywhere. And in that hour when he was born there was heard a voice of many*

invisible beings saying with one accord "Amen". And the light itself which was born increased and darkened the light of the sun with the brightness of its shining. And this cave was filled with bright light together with a most sweet odour. This light was born just as dew descends on the earth from heaven. For its odour is more fragrant than any aroma of ointments.

And I stood there stupefied and amazed, and fear seized me. For I was looking upon the intense brightness of the light which was born. But the light itself gradually withdrawing, became like a child, and in a moment became a child as children are customarily born. And I took courage and bent down and touched him, and took him up in my hands with great fear, and was seized with terror because he had no weight like other children who are born. And I looked at him and there was no defilement in him, but he was in all his body shining as in the dew of the most high God, light to carry, radiant to behold. And while I wondered greatly because he did not cry as new-born babes are accustomed to cry, and while I held him and looked at his face, he smiled at me with the most sweet smile, and opened his eyes and looked sharply on me. And suddenly there came forth from his eyes a great light like a brilliant flash of lightning.

The Gospel of Thomas has Jesus saying:

He who shall find the interpretation of these words shall not taste of death.

Jesus said: He who seeks, let him not cease seeking until he finds; and when he finds he will be troubled, and if he is troubled he will be amazed, and he will reign over the All.

Jesus said: If those who lead you say unto you: Behold, the Kingdom is in heaven, then the birds of the heaven will be before you. If they say unto you: It is in the sea, then the fish will be before you. But the Kingdom is within you, and it is outside of you. When you know yourselves, then shall you be known, and you shall know that you are the sons of the living Father. But if you do not know yourselves, then you are in poverty, and you are poverty.

Jesus said: The man aged in his days will not hesitate to ask a little child of seven days about the place of life, and he shall live. For there are many first who shall be last, and they shall become a single one

Jesus saw some infants at the breast. He said to his disciples: These little ones at the breast are like those who enter into the kingdom. They said to him: If we then be children, shall we enter the kingdom? Jesus said to them: When you make the two one, and when you make the inside as the outside, and the outside as the inside, and the upper side as the lower; and when you make the male and the female into a single one, that the male be not male and the female female; when you make eyes in the place of an eye, and a hand in place of a hand, and a foot in place of a foot, an image in place of an image, then shall you enter the kingdom.

Jesus said: I shall choose you, one out of a thousand, and two out of ten thousand, and they shall stand as a single one.

His disciples said: Teach us concerning the place where thou art, for it is necessary for us to seek after it. He said to them: He that hath ears, let him hear. There is a light within a man of light, and it gives light to the whole world. If it does not give light, there is darkness.

His disciples said: On what day wilt thou be revealed to us, and on what day shall we see thee? Jesus said: When you unclothe yourselves and are not ashamed, and take your garments and lay them beneath your feet like little children, and tread upon them, then shall ye see the Son of the living One, and ye shall not fear.

Jesus said: From Adam to John the Baptist there is none born of woman who is higher than John the Baptist, so that his eyes will not be broken. But I have said, He who shall be among you as a little one shall know the kingdom, and shall be higher than John.

Throughout His ministry, Jesus preached that people must be *born again*, which in Aramaic means to become like a child. Why this emphasis on the child-like state? The Gospels record the words of Jesus concerning His sermons on children (Matt. 18:1–5):

At the same time came the disciples unto Jesus, saying, Who is the greatest in the kingdom of heaven?

And Jesus called a little child unto him, and set him in the midst of them,

And said, Verily I say unto you, Except ye be converted, and become as little children, ye shall not enter into the kingdom of heaven.

Whosoever therefore shall humble himself as this little child, the same is greatest in the kingdom of heaven.

And whoso shall receive one such little child in my name receiveth me.

Again from Matthew (19:13–15):

Then were there brought unto him little children, that he should put his hands on them, and pray: and the disciples rebuked them.

But Jesus said, Suffer little children, and forbid them not, to come unto me: for of such is the kingdom of heaven.

And he laid his hands on them, and departed thence.

Undoubtedly, Jesus's words reflect those of Isaiah, who writes about the coming kingdom (11:6–9): *The wolf also shall dwell* with the lamb, and the leopard shall lie down with the kid; and the calf and the young lion and the fatling together; and a little child shall lead them.

The Apocryphon, or Secret Book, of John, though the extant text is badly mutilated, records a revelation made by Christ in reply to questions from John, where we see Christ assuming the form of a child. This again shows one of the primary forms in which Christ appears to instruct the human race:

> *But it came to pass one day, when John the brother of James was come up—these are the sons of Zebedee—when he was come up to the Temple, there came to him a Pharisee named Arimanias, and said to him: "Where is thy master, in whose train thou wast?" He said to him: "Whence he came, thither is he returned again." Then spake the Pharisee to him: "Through deceitful paths he led you astray, this Nazarene. He hath hardened your hearts and turned you away from the traditions of your fathers." When I heard this, I turned away from the sanctuary to the mountain, to a solitary place, and with great sorrow in my heart I thought: 'How then was the Saviour appointed and why was he sent into the world by his Father who sent him? And who is his Father? And of what kind is that aeon to which we shall go? He said to us: 'This aeon hath assumed the form of that everlasting aeon.' But he did not teach us about it, of what kind it is." Straightway, as I thus thought, the heavens opened and the whole creation shone forth in a light that is not earthly and the whole world began to tremble. I was afraid, and cast myself down. And lo, there appeared to me a child. But I saw the form as an old man, in whom is light. I looked upon him and understood not this marvel. If it is a unity with many forms in consequence of this light, do their forms appear through themselves or through one another or, if it is one, how then does it have threefold appearances? He said to me: "John, why are thou in doubt,*

> when I come to thee? For indeed this is not strange to thee. But be not faint-hearted, for I am he who is with you always. I am the Father; I am the Mother, I am the Son. I am the eternally Existing, the Unmixable, for there is none who mingles himself with him. Now am I come to reveal to thee what is, what was, and what shall be, that thou mayest know the invisible things like the visible, and to instruct thee concerning the perfect man. But now lift up thy countenance and come, hear and understand what I shall say today, that thou for thy part may proclaim it to thy fellow-spirits, who are of the race that does not waver, of the perfect Man, and to those who are able to perceive."

Another apocryphal text, the Acts of John, which escaped burning under Pope Leo the Great and again three hundred years later under the Nicene Council of 787, records the little novels concerned with the Apostles. John's preaching of the Gospel includes an interesting episode where Christ comes first in the guise of a Child, and then as an older figure. These little allegories teach us that Christ appeared to the Apostles in different forms:

> For when he had chosen Peter and Andrew, who were brothers, he came to me and to my brother James, saying, "I need you; come with me!" And my brother said this to me, "John, what does he want, this child on the shore who called us?" And I said, "Which child?" And he answered me, "The one who is beckoning to us." And I said, "This is because of the long watch we have kept at sea. You are not seeing straight, brother James. Do you not see the man standing there who is handsome, fair and cheerful-looking?" But he said to me, "I do not see that man, my brother. But let us go, and we will see what this means."

> And when we had brought the boat to land we saw how he also helped us to beach the boat. And as we left the place, wishing to follow him, he appeared to me again as rather bald-headed but with a thick, flowing beard, but to James as a young man whose

beard was just beginning. So we wondered both of us about the meaning of the vision we had seen. Then as we both followed him we became gradually more perplexed about this matter.

Another time he took me and James and Peter to the mountain where he used to pray, and we saw on him a light such that a man, who uses mortal speech, cannot describe what it was like.

I will tell you another glory, brethren; sometimes when I meant to touch him I encountered a material, solid body; but at other times again when I felt him, his substance was immaterial and incorporeal, and as if it did not exist at all.

The diverse forms of Christ are dealt with again in the Revelation of the Mystery of the Cross from the same Acts of John:

And so I saw him suffer, and did not wait by his suffering, but fled to the Mount of Olives and wept at what had come to pass. And when he was hung upon the Cross on Friday, at the sixth hour of the day there came a darkness over the whole earth. And my Lord stood in the middle of the cave and gave light to it and said, "John, for the people below in Jerusalem I am being crucified and pierced with lances and reeds and given vinegar and gall to drink. But to you I am speaking, and listen to what I speak. I put into your mind to come up to this mountain so that you may hear what a disciple should learn from his teacher and a man from God."

And when he had said this, he showed me a Cross of Light firmly fixed, and around the Cross a great crowd, which had no single form; and in the Cross was one form and the same likeness. And I saw the Lord himself above the Cross, having no shape but only a kind of voice; yet not that voice which we knew, but one that was sweet and gentle and truly the voice of God, which said to me, "John, there must be one man to hear these things from me; for I need one who is ready to hear. This

Cross of Light is sometimes called Logos by me for your sakes, sometimes mind, sometimes Jesus, sometimes Christ, sometimes a door, sometimes a way, sometimes bread, sometimes seed, sometimes resurrection, sometimes Son, sometimes Father, sometimes Spirit, sometimes life, sometimes truth, sometimes faith, sometimes grace; and so it is called for men's sake.

But what it truly is, as known in itself and spoken to us, is this: it is the distinction of all things, and the strong uplifting of what is firmly fixed out of what is unstable, and the harmony of wisdom, being wisdom in harmony. But there are places on the right and on the left, powers, authorities, principalities and demons, activities, threatenings, passions, devils, Satan and the inferior root from which the nature of transient things proceeded.

This Cross then is that which has united all things by the word and which has separated off what is transitory and inferior, which has also compacted all things into one. But this is not that wooden Cross which you shall see when you go down from here; nor am I the man who is on the Cross, I whom now you do not see but only hear my voice. I was taken to be what I am not, I who am not what for many others I was; but what they will say of me is mean and unworthy of me. Since then the place of my rest is neither to be seen nor told, much more shall I, the Lord of this place, be neither seen nor told.

The multitude around the Cross that is not of one form is the inferior nature. And those whom you saw in the Cross, even if they have not yet one form—not every member of him who has come down has yet been gathered together. But when human nature is taken up, and the race that comes to me and obeys my voice, then he who now hears me shall be united with this race and shall no longer be what he now is, but shall be above them as I am now. For so long as you do not call yourself mine, I am not what I am; but if you hear me, you also as hearer shall be as I am, and I shall be what I was, when you are as I am with myself; for from me you are what I am. Therefore ignore the many and despise those who are outside the mystery; for you must know that I am wholly with the Father, and the Father with me.

You therefore, beloved, must also be persuaded, that it is not a man that I exhort you to worship, but God unchangeable, God invincible, God who is higher than all authority and all power and elder and stronger than all angels and all that are called creatures and all aeons. So if you hold fast to him and are built up upon him, you shall possess your soul indestructible.

Extracts from the uncanonical but illuminating Acts of Peter, the chapter on Peter's miracles, describes the variety of forms taken by Christ:

And when prayer was made by all, the room in which they were shone as if with lightning, such as shines in the clouds. Yet it was not such light as is seen by day, but ineffable, invisible, such as no man could describe, a light that shone on us so brightly that we were senseless with bewilderment, and called upon the Lord and said, "Have mercy on us thy servants, Lord. Let thy gift to us, Lord, be such as we can endure; for this we can neither see nor endure." And as we lay there, there stood there only those widows, which were blind. But the bright light which appeared to us entered into their eyes and made them see.

Then Peter said to them, "Tell us what you saw." And they said, "We saw an old man, who had such a presence as we cannot describe to you"; but others said, "We saw a growing lad"; and others said, "We saw a boy who gently touched our eyes, and so our eyes were opened." So Peter praised the Lord, saying, "Thou alone art God the Lord, to whom praise is due. How many lips should we need to give thanks to thee in accordance with thy mercy? So, brethren, as I told you a little while ago, God is greater than our thoughts, as we have learnt from the aged widows, how they have seen the Lord in a variey of forms."

Jesus speaks of a Second Coming, as recorded in the canonical Gospel of John (14:27):

Let not your heart be troubled, neither let it be afraid. Ye have heard how I said unto you, I go away, and come again unto you. If ye loved me, ye would rejoice, because I said, I go unto the Father: for my Father is greater than I. . . . And I will pray the Father, and he shall give you another Comforter, that he may abide with you for ever: even the Spirit of truth; whom the world cannot receive, because it seeth him not, neither knoweth him: but ye know him; for he dwelleth with you, and shall be in you. I will not leave you comfortless: I will come to you.

Chapter 12 of the Book of Revelation (deciphered in Codex II, vol. 2, of the Sacred Teachings of Light) touches on the Second Coming of Christ. Again the allegorical use of the title of *Child* is employed to depict Christ come again (Rev. 12:1–5):

And there appeared a great wonder in heaven; a woman clothed with the sun, and the moon under her feet, and upon her head a crown of twelve stars:

And she being with child cried, travailing in birth, and pained to be delivered,

And there appeared another wonder in heaven; and behold a great red dragon, having seven heads and ten horns, and seven crowns upon his heads.

And his tail drew the third part of the stars of heaven, and did cast them to the earth: and the dragon stood before the woman which was ready to be delivered, for to devour her child as soon as it was born.

And she brought forth a man child, who was to rule all nations with a rod of iron: and her child was caught up unto God. and to his throne.

All the accounts of the infancy stories show that Christ manifested to humankind following the resurrection in various forms—oftentimes as a child. During the earthly sojourn, Christ manifested as the prophet Jesus in human form. Once Jesus was released from the earth, Christ was not limited to that form anymore. We thus see that Christ, as the Image of God, is universal and able to take on varied forms while instructing members of the human race—something that occurred rather frequently during the era of the First Corning. The Christian evangelists predicted the Second Coming and firmly believed in it. They did not know the day of His coming or the form He would assume. We can only search out scripture for a clue. The oft-mentioned Gnostic expressions of the twin-savior, the Child of the Child, or Christ's Christ, suggest that the Second Coming would be an extension of the First Coming and, therefore, related to it. This was one of the key teachings of the Gospel. The evangelists looked forward to the event as the fulfillment of the promise of Jesus, who prophesied a Second Coming that would amend and supplement that which had previously been given. The apocalyptic writers used the usual, flowery symbology to describe the event (a literal translation would have Jesus appearing out of the clouds accompanied by a loud clap of thunder and trumpets to judge the living and the dead). They predicted the beginning of a new cycle of salvation that would come at a critical time of the universe when the Church and the whole world would be in apostasy.

It does no good for man to speculate on spiritual matters. The Second Coming is dictated and governed by God. We can expect a total regeneration of Christendom that will spread to all humankind, not by means of cosmic phenomena, but by people teaching other people with Cosmic assistance, just as was done 2,000 years before. To be sure, there will be an upheaval in heaven as the Powers of Light marshal themselves against the Powers of Darkness. But this upheaval will be ultradimensional and not visible in the material universe, at least not initially, but people will suffer turmoil within their spirits.

11: THE SECRET CHURCH AT WORK

There is a new light cast upon Christendom. The living Gospel has been repossessed and amended. The errors of the established Churches are to be corrected and brought to the attention of every Christian. Above all, the individual is being put into direct contact with the manifesting cosmic Christ, shed again upon the earth under divine guidance, without which there can be absolutely no comprehension of the Christian message as given by Jesus and the original Apostles. The Second Advent, which was prophesied ages ago in the early Christian Community, has dawned. This means that the Community is being regenerated by Christ, as opposed to any form of revival engineered by a human mind. The reappearance of Christ on earth has fulfilled Christianity just as Christianity fulfilled the old Law of Judaism, and it also fulfills other world religions. As the age of grace under Jesus was separate from observance of the Law, the supplemental teachings or amendments to Christianity are separate from the new covenant of neo-Christianity. That a new community must be formed out of the old, for purity's sake, is taught in the Synoptic Gospels, which tell us that new wine must not be put into old skins, lest the skins burst and the new wine be lost. As history proclaims, when the new teaching of Christianity was absorbed into the old religions and mixed with the law, the Light of God was withdrawn. Therefore, God's Law manifesting through a new community will replace the old.

The deciphering of the encoded writings of the New Testament and other Christian scripture has been undertaken by new authority under Christ. Not all of the teachings have been committed to the written word, for much is given orally to those undertaking training in the New Ministry. The purpose of this volume is to reveal to Christians the meaning of New Testament writings and, above all, to announce to Christendom that Christ has come again into the world to fulfill the Christian message inaugurated by Jesus two thousand years ago. From Codex I of the Sacred Teachings of Light, *Jamil: The Child Christ*, we have Christ's words (25:8):

> *The Word lives in the Spirit of Christ. The Cross lives in God's New Sun. We have come to release the Christians and the peoples of other religions from bondage to words they do not understand. Too long have our brethren been led astray by those who preach from The Books, not understanding the message. For I say unto you that God summons man to live the Holy Word. We will give a supplement and open the Book of Life and all the peoples and nations of the world shall understand the hidden meaning of Scripture now given to mankind in the last and final age.*

This is the news that all Christians everywhere have been waiting for—a message that every Christian will want to hear. The new teaching is being disseminated quietly throughout the world, much the same as in the early Church in the beginning. Therefore, the new community of Christ is a secret, closed community, as it was in the beginning.

The Seals of the Book of Life, which have remained hidden since the Gospel that informed the New Testament writings was given to the world through Jesus and His disciples, have been opened. The New Ministry is dedicated to furthering the divine plan revealed by Christ. According to the old-world religions, and Judaism in particular, the First Coming of Christ was considered a heresy; nevertheless, the old world was changed by the new teachings, given by Christ (as Jesus), which fulfilled and amended the old Law. In a similar way, the Second Coming of Christ will unify the present Christian world (with all its fragmented interpretations that create separate Churches and theological differences) into a fellowship with God through a New Ministry supervised directly by Christ. The new teachings do not oppose the old, nor should the old oppose them. On the contrary, the old, or currently existing, teachings can ill afford to disregard the new supplemental teachings and amendments, which have been given to fulfill God's Church, if religion is to have any meaning in the future, or if religion is to take humankind on the return path to the Godhead.

A new age has dawned on Christendom. A new and vital prophetic message has come, which will renew and rebuild Christian communities and unite Christians with people of all faiths everywhere, as never before. The new Gospel of Christ teaches us how to live a new life in which fellowship with God is possible through a radically new kind of religious expression—not dogmatic, but progressive, in structure yet under the guidance of God instead of humans.

An entirely New Ministry and a new Christ-structure based on the new teachings given by Christ is emerging, which will be entirely removed from the official dictates of the established Church hierarchy representing the Churches of the old dispensation, much the same as primitive Christianity set itself apart from the Jewish hierarchy at Jerusalem. Salvation is given to humankind from God through Christ. Every human being is heir to this salvation. It comes through new birth made possible not through the reading of Scripture nor the simple belief in Jesus nor by the performance of ritual or ceremony but by the impregnation of the individual's spiritual consciousness by God's knowledge, giving new life and immortality. Each individual must experience this new birth for himself or herself before fellowship with God is possible.

God, through Jesus, as Christ, promised a new world for humanity, one in which death and sickness would be banished forever. It failed to materialize because the teachings were rejected and people failed to regenerate themselves as new spiritual beings under God through Christ. It did not fail because Christ's teachings were found wanting. It failed only in that the greater portion of humanity rejected the reality. It is the object of the New Ministry to inform and instruct Christians in the amendments and revelations given to Christendom through the new community of men and women being trained in the new teachings.

This ministry is restoring what was lost to the Christian religion, extending the amendments and supplements necessary for the fulfillment of the faith, as well as bringing forth a new and vital message. This message demands that Christians everywhere amend the old ways of faith, as the Hebrews were obliged to amend the old Law during the ministry of Jesus, and accept the redeeming grace of God. Those who accept and practice this new Gospel will go on to form a vital new community of men and women ordained to a new ministry in Christ, dedicated to living the teachings and establishing a new world under the spiritual direction of God.

The new community is as dedicated to the creation of a new world as were the original Christians. This is being made possible by a universal fellowship representing a new spiritual nation drawn from all the nations of the world, recognizing only God as their ruler, yet living within the established social customs and laws of their homelands—as long as such laws do not interfere with God's ordinances.

The fellowship is bringing forth highly evolutionized individuals endowed with special insight and enlightened by Christ, which gives them a new authority to teach the message to Christendom and the whole world. Animated by Christ, they are, in short, immortal beings existing in the material world for the sole purpose of uplifting their human brethren from the common ills of ignorance that breed suffering and death. They are bound together by both oral and scriptural traditions, inspired by the living Spirit of God working in their midst, and moved to bring forth a cosmic religion that is untouchable by the wills of human beings. Needless to say, such a religious institution is unlike previous religions known to humankind, not only because it is the ultimate or final religion inspired by God and revealed by Christ, and thus aided by supracosmic agencies, but because it is the last opportunity for humankind to restore the world to Light.

Above all, the new community is instructing members of the human family how to experience their divinity in the here and now and how to share in their immortal nature, thereby living a more meaningful existence beyond the limitations of the physical mind/body. By so doing, everyone contributes to the overall good of the universe in harmony with God's plan.

Organized Christianity failed Christ in many ways, mainly because it failed to bring to humankind the spiritual message of God, which could have lifted it above materialistic attitudes into a spiritual life of righteousness. World peace will never be possible until humankind takes the return path to God. Humans are first and foremost spiritual beings whose only reasons for existence are to live in the image of God and to restore their world to what it was in the beginning. Sickness, suffering, war, and death are the result of ignorance of this spiritual heritage. God never intended such a life for humanity.

If humanity fails in this final effort to change its ways and bring the world under the dominion of God, then God will abandon humankind to its own grievous ways, which will result in the negation of our parent sun and the consummation of the world by fire, as prophesied by the holy prophets.

12: THE NEW REVELATIONS OF CHRIST

Two thousand years ago the image of God called Christ appeared to the Jews as a simple carpenter in Galilee. Jesus's message was rejected and His teachings eventually lost. Again the image of God has appeared, this time as a little Child come to the Gentiles. He has appeared to individuals of the Christian tradition who are capable of understanding the message, recording it, and disseminating it throughout Christendom and the world.

The Christian religion has failed to bring peace and enlightenment to the world because its members have not been able to exemplify the primary message of Christ: to love God and walk with Him in fellowship. Such love is not possible by means of the rational mind or the human will or senses. It is only by spiritual evolvement that human consciousness develops to the degree where humans, as superior enlightened beings, can love God and all humankind. This evolvement involves a new birth that can result in the restoration of humans as spiritual beings governed by God.

It is a nonmaterial, spiritual energy that conceives a new birth and nourishes the new spiritual being. No human effort alone can bring about this birth; for, like physical procreation, which brings about new birth through electrochemical means made possible by the contact between a man and woman, it is a process that involves God's energy and Light implanted within the person. This process is immutable and not subject to human control.

The spiritual energy, sent by God and now irradiating the planet Earth through the New Sun of Righteousness, envelops the physical world as the spiritual body envelops the physical body. This spiritual energy, however, will not of itself bring about the regeneration of humankind. The spiritual energy, with its spiritual intelligence, must be utilized and converted into the divine food by the spiritual potential (the spiritual body) of the human to bring about the new birth and development of the Light body. The way or process by which the spiritual energy is utilized or experienced by the individual is the Gospel taught by Christ. The Gospel may be learned or experienced by all who wish to avail themselves of it. Since this process is of divine and not of human origin, and spiritual energy does not come from within the individual but from God, spiritual birth cannot be realized through meditation, therapy, prayer, or any technique that is of the mind or physical or rational senses. It can only come from God through Christ—the Image of God that signifies love and life. This is the whole meaning of the Christian message.

Love is the only force that can change people and the world to prevent disorder, anarchy, and a return to the old-world religions with their emphasis on sorcery, witchcraft, calling forth spirits, and demonology. If the black arts, which popular Christianity eliminated to a large degree are allowed to flourish again, the old gods and entities that have remained sleeping will regain their energies and reappear. The world will again be under the rule of powerful forces that would again blot out the message of Christ. Humans must live by Light and accept the amendments for the life of Light or this world will fall into an age of Darkness more terrible than they can possibly imagine.

Christians who may be disenchanted with organized Christianity must not abandon the Church, laboring as it is under apostasy, or attempt to find enlightenment in the old-world religions. Christians are, by their own conscience, obligated to band together under the new, inspiring power of Christ and create an International Community of Christ that can lead the world to greater religious expression than ever before in the history of the planet.

The physical or material world will eventually perish as the physical or material body perishes. Since humans can live in both worlds until death claims the material body, it is imperative that humankind learn to reshape its social structures in accordance with the new events come from God.

The message brought by the Child Christ, who dwelt among us for a time in the flesh as the image of God, announces the Gospel and teaches humankind how to participate in its spiritual immortality. Unless the spiritual nature of humankind responds to and nourishes the spiritual Sun given for their benefit, then their life on this planet will come to an end. Therefore, the New Community authorized by Christ is governed by spiritual law and order for the constructive rebuilding of what has been lost.

The Child Christ taught for a period of three years, after which He returned to the Worlds of Light from where He came. Those who did not know Him or His radiant glory, those unfamiliar with the entire story, or, especially, those steeped in the traditional teachings who would relegate Christ to a historical figure to be worshiped, instead of recognizing Him as a living force that can be shared by all Christians, might very well judge the Child, as Jesus was judged. As with the message of Jesus, what is important is the message revealed by God through the Child Christ and the

Sacred Teachings of Light that have been entrusted into the hands of the Guardians of Light, in the New Community established by and authorized by His person. These teachings are preserved in several Codices, which include the story of the life and teachings of the Child Christ; the necessary material for the Decoding of the New Testament and the Revelation; the Amendments and Supplemental Revelations to the Christian religion; and the directives for the new International Community of Christ, and the training of ministers for the New, or Second, Advent.

The following excerpts are taken from *Jamil: The Child Christ*, Codex I of the Sacred Teachings of Light (27:6–11, 13, 15–18) used as a scriptural text by members of the Community. These beautiful passages concern the new revelations and commands of God through Christ to His regenerated Church and make very clear to us today that popular translations of the standard New Testament writings, or even the recovery of lost scrolls, is not the means to an understanding of the lost Gospel of Christ. Our understanding of such a Gospel can only be realized through the appearance of Christ who must first give and then oversee the message, as was done in the beginnings of the first Christian ministry.

> *And the risen Child said: The incarnation of God the Father is come to the world through the Sun of Righteousness, healing and sustaining the human family, and restoring the Life of Righteousness. As the seed of man enters the womb of woman and life cometh forth, so shall a heavenly Seed enter the spirits of men and women, and a new birth shall occur. And the life thereof shall be of God. And death shall not claim this new Body of Light and the Spiritual Consciousness therein. And the Christ transmitted in the Sun of Righteousness, and indirectly in all living things, down to the smallest atom and particle, shall incarnate within the soul of mankind. And every man and every woman shall know that they are one with the Godhead, divine and immortal. . . .*

The Incarnation of Christ as a Universal Spiritual Force is not the property of any one religion, or of any one man or woman. Christ is the Consciousness of God the Father, who gives life to his spiritual beings as did your parents, for you were not self-generated, which proud men forget in their selfish lives, losing sight of their spiritual origins. Know you that the spiritual senses are as different from the material senses as man is from God who gave him life. No person can commune with God by means of the physical senses. It is for this reason that mankind has misunderstood the Prophets, for they are unable to comprehend God, having fallen away from the Life of Righteousness.

These Prophets of Righteousness came to teach man a Righteous Spiritual Life, as God intended the life of man to be. They were raised up by Christ who quickened their spirit and gave it life as does a parent. By these means they were able to communicate with God and interpret His sayings to man's Christ Consciousness. There are among men and women of your Christian faith those who believe that by worshipping Jesus, or by adhering to rituals, dogma or other matters of faith and belief, they will be saved. This is in error. It is not by faith or belief that man is redeemed from death. If the spiritual faculties be not developed, or given life, man fails to share the divine life. I say unto you, how can there be life if man and woman do not propagate? They think, by reason of their rational minds, that spiritual life is an occurrence comparable to the theories of their scientists who say that life is a thing of chance, an accident or trick of fate. Has any man observed an unlawful universe where there is life? Is not all governed by some law or guiding force? Know that the spiritual universe is lawful, governed and guided. Know that spiritual life is given by a new birth of body and consciousness.

Priests and ministers of your faith claim to be the direct successors of Jesus and the Apostles. They believe their teachings, based on the Holy Books, to be the Word of God. But I say unto you that the Christian message was lost to the world soon after the judicial murder of Jesus and his immediate disciples. The clergy would have the laity believe that the shedding of Jesus' blood was for the redemption of man, and a necessary sacrifice to God. Around this teaching was built a religion which conceals the true message. I speak to you in words you can understand, for you are of Christian tradition. Know, then, that the Church of the old dispensation fulfilled the earlier Hebrew tradition. Since the beginning of time, God the Father, has revealed through his glorified Prophets spiritual wisdom that would satisfy man's longing for unity with God. The Christian tradition, and the Hebrew tradition before it, nourished guardians of holy teachings now lost to the world. No book contains the true message. No scripture alone can support a religion without the living Prophets. Look around you. Where are they today?

A New Community shall come into being as a fulfillment to the Christian Church. It shall be truly universal, valid for any man or woman who longs to experience God through a new, spiritual birth, regardless of his or her religious tradition. And a new race shall grow up, nourished by the Light of Christ manifesting in the Sun of Righteousness. And this Community shall go out into the world, at an appointed time, and instruct the Christians in the New Advent, revealing the Sacred Teachings which shall be trusted into their care for dissemination to that portion of mankind who shall receive them. The Seals shall be opened and the teachings revealed to all the religions of the world. And if any mortal or Church leader challenges this authority, the Community shall say unto them that a New Creation is coming; yea, it begins now—a world of Truth and Life. None can stay the rays of Christ in the Sun of Righteousness. It is for each man and woman to choose whether they shall live in the Light. God seeks to immortalize the whole of the human family, but men reject new teachings; they ask for signs, for proof, for miracles, not realizing the spiritual birth afforded is the Miracle of Miracles.

Be ever mindful that the destiny of the world depends upon righteous men and women, for they alone can sustain the Sun of Righteousness and the Universal Christ from going out and darkening the world at the moment of a New Creation. Teachers of former times failed in their efforts to sustain the spiritual Sun of which I speak. Think not that the Prophets, abused in person, and whose teachings have been corrupted by wicked and selfish men, are content. They cry out to God to assist them and he has heard their appeals by sending into the world the unified energies of each and every one, which forms the Universal Christ. . . .

It is proper that men know that the divine Self is immortal and co-existent with God the Father. Instruction in this rebirth mustneeds be overseen by teachers unified into a whole, living organism of Light animated by Christ. Go forth and build the order, ordaining such that qualify in the teachings. Above all, unite the order as you see this heavenly effort united on high. Go forth knowing that I go with you in company with the Heavenly Host. Let all men know that the spirit of Christ, and the Sun of Righteousness—the Bread of Life—shine on all nations and peoples equally. In this way they will understand our purpose. Seek not to convince men through argument or appeal to their rational minds; speak instead of the spirit; teach them the way through the Light. . . .

Only those who eat the fruit of God shall be sustained, those others shall continue as before; yea, shall perish in the end, because they chose to live in ignorance of God, serving artificial and lesser gods. In this Great Age of Light every living thing shall be at peace with one another. Think not that the Reign of God shall commence at once. Perfection requires patience and time in the world. There shall be great conflict between the Powers of

Light and the Powers of Darkness. Take care that those blessed ones who will follow the teachings be not led astray by Beings of Darkness fallen from grace. This is the great spiritual war spoken of in former times. Already these forces are at work; the Anti-Christs who would abuse the sun and the energies thereof and the God mingled therein, to punish the Children of Light as they have done in ancient times. Be on guard, and teach against them, for they prevent man from returning to God.

From the beginning God caused the True Religions to come into the world under different names. These religions sought to restore moral order in the world and lead mankind towards Universal Brotherhood. Today moral order, in the individual and among nations, has been replaced by selfishness and a fear that spreads around the world. Anarchy threatens on a level never before known. Terrestrial concepts have replaced celestial concepts. Priests of God have been replaced by priests of the earth, men who would abuse the resources of the earth and the universe for vainglorious ends, and by so doing invade and impose themselves upon the Kingdom of God. The end result shall be revolution in society and a universe in rebellion, causing earthquakes, floods, famines, plagues and wars. Human existence shall perish if the madness created by the Powers of Darkness, seeking to exterminate the race, does not end. And if man continues blindly ahead to his own destruction, then we shall make a place for the Community, as provided to peoples in times past, and it shall survive the disorder.

In this last and final age of the world, the Universal Religion, the true religion, has come one more time from the mouth of God the Father manifest through the Living Christ and the Sun of Righteousness. And the sign is the Cross of Enlightenment, which shall be seen by all peoples by means of their spiritual sight. Man may be regenerated because of this Religion, turning from destructive ways and regaining The Way to salvation. Many religious and civil leaders, believing that things will continue as before, shall try to impose themselves in the Era of Christ by clinging to the old and attempting to tear down the new. Know that they have no authority over this Religion. Those who would speak against the Apostles or Ministers of this Religion cannot darken God's Light which is irresistible and more powerful than worldly powers. It comes to alleviate the ills of the world and is, therefore, truly universal. All Prophets of all ages—the Holy Spiritual Order of Elders —who have risen in the Light shall manifest in the Sun with Christ. They do this to restore man, their Younger Brother, who has lost his way.

The words that I speak, or may speak, are limited by your own understanding. Therefore, let the Word of God speak to your Spiritual Consciousness so that you may understand. And let all humankind listen to the Word. Fear no evil save the Darkness of which I speak.... Remember that Light gives Life: Death comes from Darkness.

The Word of God is the Supreme Authority over humankind. Two thousand years ago Jesus the Christ was judged because people questioned His authority. His condemnation and eventual crucifixion resulted in the loss of His Gospel, leaving humankind to grope in darkness over the centuries. Now the Word of God has manifested again to humankind in the form of a little Child who has endowed us with the same Gospel from God as that brought by Jesus. It is this Gospel and what it can do for the individual that is of paramount importance. It can regenerate His Church and bring forth a new world and a new race of humans animated by Christ.

It may be that members of Christ's New Ministry will be condemned by a suspicious humanity who, being caught up in the traditional teachings of the established Churches, will find it difficult to give up the old ways. If the Second Coming of Christ is rejected as was the First Coming, the loss to humankind will be irretrievable; the Light will surely go out, and the world will be cast into a darkness from which it may never recover.

It rests with Christians, who have for so long judged the Jews for rejecting Christ at His First Advent, to accept the message of Christ at His Second Advent. Those who fail to acknowledge the message cannot in good conscience call themselves Christians and must be judged even more harshly than the ancients, for Christendom has long awaited the Second Coming of Christ as its heritage. The acceptance of the New Advent does not mean that Jesus need be replaced by "another" Christ. Indeed, Christ is one, as is God, but assumes many forms. It is the Gospel that people must live if they are to inherit immortality. Those who are emotionally dependent upon Jesus, the man, have missed the whole message of Christ.

The benefits of Christ's revelation of the Redeeming Grace of God bestowed upon a needful humanity are the ennoblement of humanity and the illumination of a person's entire being. To judge the form that Christ assumes when appearing to humankind, to reject the new way while clinging to the old, is one thing, but to reject the blessings of the Gospel and the immortality of one's Godly nature from the God that gave it is quite another. It would most assuredly indicate that humanity has degenerated to a level where they are no longer capable of understanding his purpose in the world: from such as these God shall turn away forever. But, those who would walk with Christ, as did the Apostles, they have only to come forth.

www.ingramcontent.com/pod-product-compliance
Lightning Source LLC
Chambersburg PA
CBHW030148100526
44592CB00009B/181